VYGOTSKY TODAY:
ON THE VERGE OF
NON-CLASSICAL PSYCHOLOGY

HORIZONS IN PSYCHOLOGY
Series Editor: James Wertsch

Cultural-Historical Development of Verbal Thinking
by Peeter Tulviste

Learning in Children: Organization and Development of Cooperative Actions
by V. V. Rubtsov

Meaning and Categorization
by Rebecca Frumkina and Alexei Mikheev

Psychophysiology of Visual Masking
by Talis Bachmann

V. M. Bekhterev's Collective Reflexology
edited by L. H. Strickland

Piotr Gal'perin: A Lifetime of Searching for the Content of Psychology
by Jacques Haenen

Russian Psychology: Past, Present and Future
edited by Elena L. Grigorenko, Patricia Ruzgis and Robert J. Sternberg

VYGOTSKY TODAY:
ON THE VERGE OF
NON-CLASSICAL PSYCHOLOGY

ALEXANDER G. ASMOLOV

Nova Science Publishers, Inc.
Commack, New York

Editorial Production: Susan Boriotti
Office Manager: Annette Hellinger
Graphics: Frank Grucci and John T'Lustachowski
Information Editor: Tatiana Shohov
Book Production: Donna Dennis, Patrick Davin, Christine Mathosian
   and Tammy Sauter
Circulation: Maryanne Schmidt
Marketing/Sales: Cathy DeGregory

Library of Congress Cataloging-in-Publication Data
Asmolov, A. G. (Aleksandr Grigor'evich)
      Vygotsky today : on the verge of non-classical psychology / Alexander G.
Asmolov.
            p.   cm.-- (Horizons in psychology)
      ISBN 1-56072-616-4
          1. Psychology--Russia (Federation)--Moscow--History--20th century. 2.
Personality and culture--Russia(Federation)--Moscow. 3. Psychology--Methodology--
History. I. Title. II. Series.
BF108.R88A86   1998   98-39083
150'.947--DC21   CIP

Copyright © 1998 by Nova Science Publishers, Inc.
        6080 Jericho Turnpike, Suite 207
        Commack, New York 11725
        Tele. 516-499-3103   Fax 516-499-3146
        e-mail: Novascience@earthlink.net
        e-mail: Novascil@aol.com
        Web Site: http://www.nexusworld.com/nova

Printed in the United States of America

CONTENTS

FOREWORD

JAMES V. WERTSCH
Department of Education
Washington University
St. Louis, MO 63130-4899, USA
(jwertsch@artsci.wustl.edu)

September, 1998

This is a little book with big and very worthwhile ambitions. Building on one of the most brilliant traditions of twentieth century psychology, Alexander Asmolov seeks to formulate an approach that transcends the limitations of today's disciplinary isolation and reductionism. The groundwork for this approach comes from the ideas of Vygotsky, but Asmolov goes well beyond these in several respects. Indeed, he has spent his career developing a perspective that incorporates the insights of figures such as D.N. Uznadze and A.N. Leontiev alongside those of Vygotsky, the result being that he has become one of the major figures in contemporary Russian psychology. In the current volume he extends his long-standing effort in important new ways.

In the chapters of this volume, Asmolov addresses one of the most complex, and at the same time productive tensions that runs throughout the writings of Vygotsky and his followers. On the one hand, a fundamental goal for Vygotsky was to formulate the ways in which human consciousness is shaped by the historical, institutional, and cultural settings in which it emerges. In contrast to implicit, often ethnocentric assumptions about universals in human mental functioning, this perspective begins from the point of view that different sociocultural settings give rise to different forms of human mental life. For example, types of reasoning characteristically found in traditional societies may be quite different than those found in modern, industrial societies, and within the latter, the forms of discourse and thought characteristic of bureaucratic institutional settings may be quite distinct from those found in other contexts such as family life or religious ceremonies. In the terminology I have sought to employ when addressing such issues, human mental life is fundamentally and inherently "socioculturally situated" (Wertsch, 1998).

In pursuing this line of argument, however, Asmolov, like Vygotsky, seeks to avoid reducing the processes involved to some kind of simple social learning, or the kind of social reductionism that concerned Dewey (Westbrook, 1991). Asmolov specifically does not want to say that sociocultural settings mechanistically determine human consciousness. For him, to recognize the power of the sociocultural setting to shape human action is not to assume that individuals simply absorb social forces in a passive manner. Instead, there is also an essential role given to the active agent.

When addressing this issue, Asmolov relies heavily on the notion of "personality." This notion is so central to his argument, yet so open to misinterpretation that it is worth spending a few moments considering just what it means. The term *personality* as used by Asmolov, Leontiev (1975), and others is a translation of the Russian term *lichnost'*. As reflected in the *Oxford Russian-English Dictionary* (Wheeler, 1972) and elsewhere, this is a perfectly appropriate translation. The first English equivalent listed in virtually all dictionaries is *personality*, and the second is *individual*.

The problem with translating *lichnost'* as *personality*, at least in texts having to do with academic psychology, is that the latter term in the North America and the UK has taken on some very clear, and limiting overtones. Over the past half century "personality psychology" has become a recognized, institutionalized subdiscipline of psychology. This subdiscipline has its own widely recognized set of founding theorists, journals, conferences, divisions of professional organizations, subdivisions of departments, and so forth assigned to it, and it is associated with an established set of psychometric tools around which entire research traditions, corporations, and other bureaucratic institutions have evolved. In other words, *personality* has taken on a particular, very definite meaning in the contemporary world of psychological research and practice in the English speaking world.

The problem for Asmolov--and many other authors as well--is that when the term *personality* turns up in an English translation of their writings, it is difficult for the reader to avoid all the conceptual baggage that attaches to this word. The point I am making here is tied to a claim that one of Vygotsky's contemporaries, M.M. Bakhtin (1985-1975), made about meaning in general. Bakhtin wrote:

The word in language is half someone else's. It becomes "one's own" only when the speaker populates it with his own intention, his own accent, when he appropriates the word, adapting it to his own semantic and expressive intention. Prior to this moment of appropriation, the word does not exist in a neutral and impersonal language (it is not, after all, out of a dictionary that the speaker gets his words!), but rather it exists in other people's mouths, in other people's contexts, serving other people's intentions: it is from there that one must take the word, and make it one's own. And not all words for just anyone submit equally easily to this appropriation, to this seizure and transformation into private property: many words stubbornly resist, others remain alien, sound foreign in the mouth of the one who appropriated them and who now speaks them, they cannot be assimilated into his context and fall out of it; it is as if they put themselves in quotation marks against the will of the speaker. Language is not a neutral medium that passes freely and easily into the private property of the speaker's intentions; it is populated--overpopulated--wit the intentions of others. (1981, pp. 293-294)

As I re-read these lines (they are some of my favorite ones in Bakhtin's writings), I am struck by how powerfully they apply to the problem we encounter when trying to translate Asmolov and other Russian authors who deal with *lichnost'*. The fact that in English language texts about psychology *personality* is "half [or in this case 90%?] someone else's" means that it is almost impossible for English speaking psychologists to read Asmolov's work in the way he intended. In the abstract we can appreciate that he wishes to address crucial issues of how active, agentive consciousness shape the individual's encounter with sociocultural settings, but every time someone steeped in North American psychological literature encounters the term *personality* it is impossible to ignore the fact that "the word does not exist in a neutral and impersonal language."

Bakhtin's point that "it is not, after all, out of a dictionary that the speaker gets his words!" hits home here since it is precisely by relying on standard Russian-English dictionaries that we have translated *lichnost'* as *personality* in the first place. Instead of being able to make sense of what Asmolov says on his own terms, this is an instance in which a word does not "submit equally easily to . . . appropriation." Instead, from Asmolov's perspective the term *personality* "stubbornly resists," "remains alien," and "cannot be assimilated into his context." Indeed, it might be better when translating *lichnost'* to allow it to "put itself into quotation marks" since that at least would provide a constant--and constantly needed--reminder that we are trying to harness *personality* to say something that runs against its usual meaning in the community of English speaking psychologists.

I have gone on at such great length on this issue not because I think *lichnost'* has been mistranslated in Asmolov's book; I know of no better way to translate it. Instead, I focus on this issue because I see it as crucial to consciously, but silently put *personality* "into quotation marks" every time we encounter in the chapters that follow. If one does not do so, one risks missing essential and very profound points in Asmolov's line of reasoning. To further complicate matters, I should note that the meaning of *lichnost'* is by no means completely different or completely unrelated to *personality* in writings on psychology in North America and the UK. Completely separate meanings would simplify our problem greatly. It is precisely the various points and degrees of overlap that make it so important to remain on our conceptual guard.

Of course the terminological point I have been making reflects a broader set of concerns about different conceptual and theoretical systems. What makes reading Asmolov's book so exciting is not that we can learn a new meaning of *personality*, instead it is that he offers us a way into an important world view of human nature and consciousness that differs in significant and insightful ways with what we are likely to encounter in Western psychology. It is a world view that stresses the importance of cultural, historical, and institutional forces when trying to understand human mental functioning, but one that also does not lose sight of the active human agent.

The point I have been trying to make is related to an observation John Dewey made over a half century ago. In 1938 he wrote, "Mankind likes to think in terms of extreme opposites. It is given to formulating its beliefs in terms of *Either-Ors*, between which it recognizes no intermediate possibilities" (p. 17). Asmolov's entire book may be read as an attempt to avoid the temptation "to think in terms of extreme opposites." His non-classical psychology rejects the assumption that one can start the analytic enterprise from the perspective of a sociocultural context, which mechanistically determines human consciousness, on the one hand, or from the perspective of an individual mind or consciousness that functions in isolation from the sociocultural world, on the other. His is a call to accept human complexity by pursuing an analysis that "lives in the middle" (Holquist, 1994). It is only by doing so that he believes we can address many of the problems we encounter in today's complicated and rapidly changing world. In my view, this is not only a correct, but a profound perspective, and we would all benefit a great deal by taking it seriously.

REFERENCES

Bakhtin, M.M. (1981). *The dialogic imagination: Four essays by M.M. Bakhtin.* Austin: University of Texas Press. (edited by M Holquist; translated by C. Emerson and M. Holquist)

Dewey, J. (1938). *Experience and education.* New York: Collier Books.

Holquist, M. (1994). The reterritorialization of the enthymeme. Paper presented at the International Conference on "Vygotsky and the Human Sciences," Moscow, Russia, September, 1994.

Leont'ev, A.N. (1975). *Deyatel'nost', soznanie, lichnost'* [Activity, consciousness, personality]. Leningrad: Izdatel'stvo Politicheskoi Literaturi. Published in English as *Activity, consciousness, personality.* Englewood Cliffs, N.J.: Prentice-Hall, 1978.

Wertsch, J.V. (1998). *Mind as action.* New York: Oxford University Press.

Westbrook, R.B. (1991) *John Dewey and American democracy.* Ithaca: Cornell University Press.

Wheeler, M. (1972) *The Oxford Russian-American dictionary.* Oxford: Clarendon Press. (B.O. Unbegaun, general editor)

The psychology of personality is a dramatic psychology. The field and the center of this drama is the struggle of personality against its own spiritual destruction. This struggle never ceases.

A.N. Leontiev

PROLOGUE

The book in front of you is the result of the author's research and reflections through the period 1974 to 1996, born mainly in the atmosphere of the faculty of psychology of Moscow State University (MSU), that deal with the destiny of the methodology of modern psychology, its becoming as an effective and constructive science of the development of human world in the changing flow of history of the nature and the society. Various aspects of the theme "Historical-Evolutionary Approach to the Psychology of Personality" and methodological principles of its elaboration can be represented by the collection of books and papers published during this period.

A general reflection on the principles of cultural-historical psychology as the base for the historical-evolutionary approach to the psychology of personality, was presented in the following articles: "Social Biography of Cultural-Historical Psychology" (In the book by L.S. Vygotsky, A.R. Luria *"Etudes on the History of Behavior"*, Moscow, 1993), *"Ecology, Psychology and Historical-Evolutionary Approach"* (Alma Mater. The High School Bulletin, 1992, No. 1); "A Non-passed Way: From the Culture of Usefulness - to the Culture of Dignity" (*Questions of Psychology*, 1990, No. 1).

The reflections on the fundamentals and some perspectives of the activity theory approach to the analysis of mental phenomena, the development of which is most closely linked to the cultural-historical psychology, were presented mainly in the articles "On the Dynamic Approach to the Psychological Analysis of Activity" (*Questions of Psychology*, 1978, No. 2, in co-authorship); "Main Principles of Psychological Analysis in Activity Theory Approach" (*Questions of Psychology*, 1982, No. 2) as well as in the textbook "*Principles of Organization of Human Memory: Systems and Activity Theory Approach to the Analysis of Cognitive Processes*" (Moscow, 1985).

The ideas elaborated in the monograph "*Activity and Set*" (Moscow, 1979) and in the article "On the Crossroads of the Study of Human Mind: Unconscious, Set, and Activity" (in: "*The Unconscious: its Nature, Functions and Methods of Research*", Tbilisi, 1985), provide a special bridge making possible the transition from the systematization of the principles of the activity theory approach in psychology to their application in the psychology of the personality.

The next and central stage of the shaping of the historical-evolutionary approach to the psychology of personality that emerged in the course of the analysis of various directions of the study of personality development in the context of cultural-historical psychology and the activity theory approach in psychology, is represented primarily in the articles: "On the Subject of the Psychology of Personality" (*Questions of Psychology*, 1983, No. 3); "Historical-Evolutionary Approach to the Understanding of Personality: Problems and perspectives" (*Questions of Psychology*, 1986, No. 1); as well as in the books "*Personality as an Object of Psychological Investigation*" (Moscow, 1984); "*Psychology of Individuality: Methodological principles of Personality Development in the Historical-Evolutionary Process*" (Moscow, 1986); "*The Psychology of Personality: The Principles of General Psychological Analysis*" (Moscow, 1990).

The final research stage was the concrete application of the historical-evolutionary activity theory approach to such a sphere of social practice as education. The key moments in the use of the possibilities of the historical-evolutionary approach in the organization of practical psychology in education, as a sort of applied human science, and in the designing of the system of the developing variable education are reflected in the collected booklet "*Practical Psychology as the Basis for the Differentiation and Individualization of Education*" (M., 1991) and in the articles "Strategy of

Variable Education: Myths and Reality" ("*Magister*", 1995, No. 1); "Education as Enhancement of Possibilities of Personality Development: From Selective Assessment - to the Developmental One" (*Questions of Psychology*, 1992, No. 1-2, in co-authorship); "Personality: psychological strategy of education " (in: *New Pedagogical Thinking*, Moscow, 1988), as well as in the brochure "*Non-standard Education in the Changing World: Cultural-Historical Perspective*" (in co-authorship, Novgorod, 1993).

The publications listed above reflect just the logic of development, rather than the chronology of the historical-evolutionary approach in the psychology of personality, developed by the author. The central meaning of these publications can be found in three books: "*Activity and Set*" (Moscow, 1979); "*The Psychology of Personality: a textbook*" (Moscow, 1990), and "*Cultural-Historical Psychology and the Construction of the Worlds*" (Moscow-Voronezh, 1996).

The general characteristics of the logic of development of this research would be incomplete without mentioning my teachers, colleagues and disciples. Only intensive discussions with them made the development of the historical-evolutionary activity theory approach in psychology possible. This research could never have been fulfilled if the author in his student days did not have the happy chance to meet Alexey Nikolayevich Leontiev and Alexander Romanovich Luria. Dialogues with them have completely determined my further path in both psychology and life. The first lessons in the devotion to psychology the author received from M. Mikhalevskaya. Goodwill and optimism from A. Zaporozhets, the soft critical irony from P. Galperin, a rare feeling of dignity with respect to people and to scientific facts of B. Zeigarnik helped the author to understand the aims to which a professional psychologist should aspire. The dream of an image of human beings, not restricted by narrow limits of rationality, has appeared in discussions with Fillip Bassin, Alexander Prangishvili, and Appolon Sherozia, as well as in absorption of Merab Mamardashvili's charming lectures.

During the research, which took twenty years, the author adhered to the school of methodology of psychology by G.M. Andreeva, Yu.B. Gippenreiter, V.V. Davydov, V.P. Zinchenko, M. Cole, I.S. Kon, A.V. Petrovsky, O.V. Ovchinnikova, O.K. Tikhomirov, N.F. Talyzina, D.I. Feldstein, and M.G. Yaroshevsky. The ethics of scientific discussion with the representatives of other schools, which despite the contrast in fundamental methodological premises recognized the competence of other scientific positions, has been developed in dialogues with L.M. Vekker, Sh.A. Nadirashvili, R.T. Sakvarelidze and I.M. Feingenberg.

Whatever passions boiled among the generation of the author, many representatives of this generation become the carriers of the Zeitgeist created by cultural-historical psychology and activity theory approach to the analysis of mental phenomena. In the first case I should name B.S. Bratus, B.M. Velichkovsky, V.K. Viliunas, A.I. Dontsov, A.N. Zhdan, V.A. Ivannikov, I.I. Iliasov, M.M. Kochenov, V.V. Petukhov, V.F. Petrenko, L.A. Petrovskaya, A.I. Podolsky, A.A. Puzyrei, V.Ya. Romanov, V.V. Rubtsov, V.I. Slobodchikov, S.D. Smirnov, V.S. Sobkin, H.T. Sokolova, A.S. Spivakovskaya, V.V. Stolin, E.V. Subbotsky, P. Tulviste, A.U. Kharash, A.G. Shmelev and B.D. Elkonin. This quite visible college has never let the author feel lonely in psychology even when he, while organizing the applied psychological service in education, found himself in worlds rather distant from the psychological community. It is necessary to especially emphasize that the idea about the role of non-adaptive activity in the historical-evolutionary process, passing through the whole work, has appeared in both mental and practical co-authorship with V.A. Petrovsky, who introduced the idea of the non-adaptive activity of personality into the science of psychology.

Only due to joint research with V.V. Abramenkova, A.M. Ailamazian, F.Ye. Vasiluk, S.N. Enikolopov, M.A. Kovalchuk, D.A. Leontiev, T.Yu. Marilova, E.E. Nasinovskaya, M.S. Nyrova, L.A. Radzikhovsky, V.V. Semenov, M.V. Tendriakova and E.I. Shliagina, the author decided to address to such different aspects of the psychology of personality, in the broad sense of the word, as social psychology of childhood, psychology of simulation games, psychology of experiencing, motivation of criminal behavior, change of social attitudes, self-actualization and self-fulfillment of personality, sociopsychological rehabilitation of personality, diagnostics of altruistic behavior, psychology of creativity in the history of culture, history of cultural-historical psychology, psychogenetics, paleopsychology and historical ethnopsychology. This work would not have come about without discussions and research with E.I.Feigenberg in which special attention was paid to the possibilities of nonverbal communications in the reeducation of a person.

The author has not only tried to teach his post-graduate students concrete analysis from the positions of a historical-evolutionary activity theory approach to different phenomena of actualgenesis and ontogenesis of personality, but he also learned from them in their Ph.D. research: "Interaction of Sets in the Process of Activity Regulation" (G.Ya. Shapirshtein, MSU, 1988); "Development and Manifestation of Humane Sets of the Personality" [on the material of donor activity] (V.V. Kolpachnikov, MSU, 1990); "Moral Decentration as a Mechanism of Personality Development" (A.V. Solomatina, MSU, 1992); "The Comic in the System of Set Regulation of Behavior" (M.V. Borodenko, MSU, 1995); "Peculiarities of the Sense Sphere of Personality in Persons with Distortions of Social Regulation of Behavior" (Yu.A. Vasilyeva, MSU, 1995).

In general, after a quarter of a century of teaching psychology on the faculty of psychology of Moscow State University and almost a decade of working with politicians, managers and teachers, the author is convinced that those philosophers and psychologists (B.M. Kedrov, A.N. Leontiev, G. Piaget) were correct, who ascribed to psychology the title of the leading field of future human social sciences.

HISTORICAL-EVOLUTIONARY APPROACH: INTRODUCTORY NOTES

In the psychology of personality the idea of a *human being as a participant in the historical-evolutionary process, carrying social roles, having a possibility to choose his/her life course, and doing this, transforming the world, the society and him/herself,* has been granted the citizenship just recently. In the context of these ideas, developed from the viewpoint of the historical-evolutionary approach, the relations between individual as the product of anthropogenesis, personality integrating social and historical experience, and individuality transforming the world can be expressed in the following way: *"Born an Individual. Becoming a Personality. Asserting an Individuality".*

The relevance of posing the problem of the development and application of the historical-evolutionary approach to psychology of personality, underlying the above view on the human being, is dictated by a number of methodological and sociocultural circumstances, that urge seeking for the regularities of transformation of biogenesis, sociogenesis, and ontogenesis during the life course and to build the subject of the psychology of personality on their basis.

The first circumstance is that in psychology we have met serious difficulties until now when attempting to outline the field of empirical facts relevant to the psychological investigation of personality. The collision of opinions between the representatives of different approaches in the psychology of personality begins already a the starting point of the psychological analysis of personality and manifests itself in the question, what is the special phenomenology of this branch of psychology? In studies on the psychology of personality, various human manifestations such as constitution and character, reaction time and volition, readiness to personality self-determination and the type of higher nervous activity, asymmetry of brain hemispheres and world view in different historical epochs, physical age and personal choice, temperament and features of national character, conformity and experiencing in critical situations, affect, stress and social attitudes, physical defect and self-consciousness etc. are interlaced. Such diversity of human manifestations in the nature and society goes along with the assumption of the existence of some one-dimensional phenomenology of personality implicitly suggested by the logic of concrete empirical research. This assumption often pushes psychologists on the path of solving illusory contradictions, while discussions sometimes remind one of a dispute of blind people who touched an elephant from different sides and put forward various versions of what they were dealing with. Implicit assumptions about the one-dimensional phenomenology of personality have been changed to attempts to collect an integral person by combining various manifestations of personality "by aspects". This leads to the illusion of integrity of the subject of the psychology of personality, though in fact there is just a mechanical conglomerate of "aspects" of different manifestations of human beings, fastened by statistical correlations.

Especially clear in the psychology of personality is also the fact that even the recognition of this or that fact is in many respects stipulated by the theoretical approach or scientific school adhered to by the scientist. What looks as an irrefutable fact for social behaviorism may be perceived as a phantom in analytical psychology, individual psychology or psychoanalysis. The tendency of growing eclecticism in hitherto irreconcilable scientific schools in psychology of personality, apparent in the recent decades, being a positive indication of a search for a constructive dialogue, has not, however, become a breakthrough to the productive conceptual synthesis of the desired subject of the psychology of personality from separate facts. This construction of the subject of psychology of personality, like in the recent past, reminds one of the building of the Tower of Babel, with one exception that the builders are now able to look at each other more peacefully and communicate in different languages in a gentle way with some hope to be understood. The dispersion of empirical data in the psychology of personality and the abundance of non-intersected theories give evidence for the many-sidedness of the phenomenology of personality and for the necessity to develop a systems approach removing methodological barriers from the way of the development of the psychology of personality.

The second circumstance, providing the necessity to establish the problem of a historical-evolutionary approach to the psychology of personality, is the need for integration of the manifestations of individual, personality and individuality, that stand behind diverse phenomena of the psychology of personality that are studied within the framework of rather independent biogenetic, sociogenetic and persogenetic orientations of modern human science.

Methodologically, it is quite reasonable to distinguish the concepts "individual" and "personality", appearing in psychology as a dichotomy (A.N. Leontiev); or in trichotomies "individual", "personality", "subject of activity" (S.L. Rubinshtein, B.G. Ananiev), "organism", "social individual", "personality" (M.G. Yaroshevsky, R. Harre). This distinction used to be discussed in psychology by K.A. Abulkhanova-Slavskaya, L.I. Antsyferova, V.S. Merlin, V.V. Stolin, A.V. Petrovsky, V.A. Petrovsky and others. This real incongruity of different hypostases of human beings in biogenesis, sociogenesis and persogenesis can push legalization of three parallel worlds in the study of personality rather than solve the problem of the common coordinate system for personality research within the framework of biogenetic, sociogenetic and persogenetic orientations (I.S. Kon).

The representatives of *biogenetic orientation* are focused on the problems of development of the human being as an individual having definite anthropogenetic properties (endowment, temperament, biological age, gender, constitution type, neurodynamic properties of the brain, organic drives etc.), which pass various stages of maturation while fulfilling in their ontogenesis the phylogenetic program of the species. The basis of individual maturation is mainly formed by adaptive processes of the organism that are studied by disciplines like psychophysiology of individual differences, psychogenetics, psychosomatics, neuropsychology, psychoendocrinology and sexology. The representatives of different schools of *sociogenetic orientation* study mainly the processes of human socialization, one's mastering of social norms and roles, acquiring social attitudes and value systems, development of social and national character of the person as a typical member of this or that community. The problems of socialization or, in a broader sense, social adjustment of a person are being developed mainly in social psychology, ethnopsychology and historical psychology. In the focus of persogenetic orientation we find the problems of activity, self-consciousness and creativity of personality, development of Self, struggle of motives, development of individual character and abilities, self-fulfillment, personal choice, incessant search of meaning in life during the individuality's life course. The study of all these manifestations of personality is connected with general psychology of personality, different aspects of which are enlightened in psychoanalysis, individual psychology, analytical psychology, humanistic psychology, personology etc.

In the separation of biogenetic, sociogenetic and persogenetic directions we see different versions of a metaphysical scheme of determination of personality development influenced by two factors - environment and heredity.

Methodological stereotypes stipulating the longevity of a dual determination scheme of personality development so far have not received a detailed critical elaboration in psychology. As a result, the dual determination scheme continues to remain that "overconscious set" (M.G. Yaroshevsky) which largely supports the break between general psychology of personality and psychology of individual differences. The separation of biogenetic, sociogenetic and persogenetic orientations also feeds numerous binary oppositions linked to the contrasting of "objectivism" and "subjectivism" in understanding of human beings, for example: "animal and/or social creature", "faceless carried of social relations and/or original individuality", "nomothetic and/or ideographic laws of the person's behavior description", "social or personal identity" and so on. The necessity to overcome the strict separation of biogenesis, sociogenesis and persogenesis into different "carriers" and to remove methodological overconscious sets in the scholars' mentality, feeding the strict differentiation of individual, personality and individuality, is the second circumstance that makes evident the relevance of the development of the historical-evolutionary approach in the psychology of personality.

The third circumstance is the *interdisciplinary status of the problem of personality* being a focus of attention of both social and natural sciences, spiritual culture and practice. Psychology and sociology, anthropology and ethnography, culturology and semiology, archaeology and philology, politology and genetics, biology and history look for ways to overcome interdisciplinary borders in the analysis of human development in natural evolution, history of society and the person's individual life. This search leads to the temptation to select just one unique scientific discipline which would possess all the truth about personality. The situation emerges here when the psychology invites "Vikings" to solve its problems and appeals to them: "Come and rule us" (A.N. Leontiev). And following such an appeal, but still more often without any, the representatives of cybernetics, biology, sociology, ethics and anthropology move into psychology to implant their understanding of personality. For example, human biology considers a human being an individual, a representative of the species Homo Sapiens having a number of essential differences from other biological species. The cybernetics reveals in human being an adaptive self-regulating system having analogues both in living and inorganic nature. Philology, dealing with, for instance, human image in an antique tragedy, speaks about a hero not burdened by feelings, who just acts as prescribed by fate. In fact, both anthropology and ethics possess a more integral image of the human being than some approaches in traditional psychology that possess "partial" pictures.

The searches for ways to overcome the crisis in the psychology of personality have resulted in the waves of its *modernization.* The representatives of these waves connect the perspectives of psychology's delivery from its own contradictions either with other related sciences or with widely spread nowadays directions of holistic (in the broad meaning) or humanistic psychology.

One of these waves can be called a wave of *anthropologization.* The productive moment of "anthropologization" in the psychology of personality, whether we apply to anthropogenesis in studying of individual-related properties of personality (A.G. Asmolov), special psychological anthropology as the basis of psychology of subjectivity (V.I. Slobodchikov) or human spiritedness in the romantic poetic anthropology (V.P. Zinchenko), is very promising as a source the value set for the search of integrity of the real person and as a protest against "partial" pictures of the human being. "Anthropologization" of the psychology of personality, however, bears serious risk to dissolve the psychology of personality's own questions in philosophical methodology and to infinitely soar over the ocean of empirical facts extracted with supreme efforts in specific areas of psychology.

Another wave is connected with *"humanization"* and *"ethics"* in the psychology of personality (B.S. Bratus, A.B. Orlov). According to B.S. Bratus, academic psychology was the psychology where the winner is always justified. It lost the spiritual, the humane in the person. Unlike academic psychology, "humanitarian" psychology still has a non-realized potential of "value setting" (not to be confused with "goal setting") which is so desired by the personality that has lost its vital ideals. But "humanitarian psychology", fed by the history of culture, religion, philology and ethics, is also trapped with the danger, to use L.S. Vygotsky's favorite saying from the New

Testament, to "render unto Caesar the things which are Caesar's; and unto God the things that are God's", thus rendering the humane in the person unto ethics and religion, while body and cognitive processes unto biology and academic psychology, say, cognitive psychology.

Finally, one more modernization wave concerning the inter-disciplinary status of personality could be described as *pragmatic and philosophical "westernization"* of the psychology of personality. The old formula "the grass is always greener on the other side of the fence", stimulated by the liberation of consciousness from the so-called "Soviet imperialism" in psychology (V. Kolga) results in a situation that looks like "pluralism at a broken wash-tub" (V.P. Zinchenko). All that has been created in Russian psychology is crossed through, and "instead" rather that "besides" the new dimension is filled by such approaches as psychosynthesiss (R. Assagioli), ontopsychology (A. Menegetti), neuro-linguistic programming (J. Grinder). Undoubtedly, the experience of these approaches is interesting for the synthesis of the psychology of personality, as well as for marking the crosspoints of humanistic and Russian psychology. Other things raise sadness: enthusiasm directed at these approaches results in the fact that in Russian psychology of personality "the baby is thrown away together with the bath water". As a result, in the overall map of searches of interdisciplinary synthesis of the ideas on personality a paradoxical situation arises: psychologists in the West, developing the methodology of humanitarian knowledge, discover L.S. Vygotsky for themselves, M.M. Bakhtin, N.A. Bernshtein, Yu.M. Lotman and S.L. Rubinshtein (see J. Gibson, M. Golder, J. Wertsch, L. Smolka, V. Matthaeus, L. Mohl, R. Harre and others), while Russian psychologists sometimes remind us of "those who do not remember kith and kin". In other words, while hitherto Western approaches in psychology were criticized through the Iron Curtain, today the methodology of humanitarian sciences in our native land is looked at quite skeptically. In fact, everything goes in circles, and the methodology of the study of personality risks turning into the "provincial secondary private-reader" psychology criticized by G.I. Chelpanov.

All the above-mentioned illustrates that the interdisciplinary status of the problem of personality appears as a necessary condition for the search of system regularities of human development in biogenesis, sociogenesis and ontogenesis rather than a ground to dissolve the psychology of personality in other natural or social sciences. It also means that in order to resolve the conflicts in the psychology of personality, the historical-evolutionary approach highlights through regularities of human development and builds, due to these regularities, a bridge between various spheres of historical and natural study of the human being, and then, being supported by the concrete methodology of psychology, "operates" with the facts in the sphere of the psychology of personality proper.

The *fourth circumstance* indicating the necessity of the development of historical-evolutionary approach to the psychology of personality is directly connected with the specificity of the historical period experienced by Russia. This period can be characterized as a period of transition from a stable to a dynamic phase in Russian history. In similar periods the person finds oneself "thrown into the historical situation of development" (by analogy with the "social situation of development" in the sense of L.S. Vygotsky), in which the traditional value system is crushed. The search for personal and group identity sharpens, the influence of a person's individual actions on the course of historical process increases. As a result, in order to develop a logic of actions aimed at passing through dramas of troubled times the psychologist is forced to design different scenarios for the situation of historical development, without restricting oneself by the famous formula "here and now".

Thereby, our time of changes brings a psychologist to the double historical trial. He should stand the test of historical sensitivity of the psychology of personality and of its participation in the changes occurring in the country. The test of historical sensitivity of psychology goes on the arena of permanent "battles for psychology in a history" (M. Block, L. Feuvre) and "battles for a history in psychology" (L.S. Vygotsky). One of the consequences of these permanent discussions about relations between psychology and history is the emergence of various hybrid disciplines such as "paleopsychology" (B.F. Porshnev), "historical psychology" (I. Meierson, J.-P. Vernan and others) and "psychohistory" (E. Eriksen, L. de Moues). At the end of the eighties a new burst of interest in interdisciplinary research has brought Russian historians and psychologists to the establishment of a standing inter-institute seminar on historical psychology (A.I. Gurevich, L.M. Batkin, G.G. Diligensky, Vyach.Vs. Ivanov, A.G. Asmolov, V.A. Shkuratov and others).

Another consequence of clearing out the relations between history and psychology is a revision of original paradigms in different areas of psychology. An impressive example of the claims of psychologists on participation in the events occurring in history is presented by an article with deliberately shocking title: "Social psychology as history", written by a well-known social psychologist K.J. Gergen. A striving for such a revision of paradigms in the social and behavioral sciences is in many respects stipulated by the intention to make one's science the one creating, rather than just studying, history. An attempt to respond to the challenge of our troubled times is just the historical-evolutionary approach in the psychology of personality, claiming to make it a constructive effective psychology, as well as the organization of psychological services based on this approach.

A list of features that highlight the reason for establishing the problem of the historical-evolutionary approach in the psychology of personality would be short and incomplete without mentioning the last but not least *fifth* circumstance. *The emphasis on the creative methodological potential of the practical psychology of personality* is both alpha and omega of the historical-evolutionary approach; it is this practical psychology that is called in the long run to help the psychology of personality, tired of different academic diseases, out of crisis. Despite its "wildness" and eclecticism, the practical psychology of personality even at early stages of its growth, constructively helps to overcome the psychology of the "partial" person (A.G. Asmolov, I.V. Dubrovina, V.A. Ivannikov, V.V. Rubtsov). From the very beginning it resists various intradiciplinary and interdisciplinary dispersion of knowledge about human development in the history of nature and society. The practical psychology of personality feels tight in the framework of developmental, educational, clinical or any other single branch of psychology. In some sense, practical psychology is doomed to "superficiality" without which any interdisciplinary synthesis is impossible. Therefore, while the representatives of academic psychology argue whether to count M.M. Bakhtin or Yu.M. Lotman as the inhabitants of the space of true psychology or to keep them out of it, labeling the former as "philologist" and the latter as "semiotician", practical psychologists, for example, already build the communication process with consideration of the dialogue theory of consciousness and semiotic theory of culture (see, for example, collected volumes: "Charting the Agenda. Educational Activity after Vygotsky. Ed. By H. Daniels, 1994; Vygotsky and Education. Instructional Implications and Applications of Sociohistorical Psychology. Ed. By L. Mohl, 1994). Thereby it is in practical psychology, where both intradiciplinary and interdisciplinary barriers, hindering the construction of the psychology of personality development, can be overcome.

A source of the methodological potential of practical psychology, which will serve as a touchstone for checking strong and weak sides of the historical-evolutionary approach, is that the object for application of its efforts is primarily a concrete person in a concrete sociohistorical situation of development. Therefore, in search of the way out of the crisis of the psychology of personality we can just repeat after Vygotsky that practical psychology is that very stone, neglected by the builders, which has become a cornerstone of the historical-evolutionary approach. The development of this approach can bring about a change in the social status of psychology in Russia and transform it into a history-making science.

MAIN OBJECTIVE, OBJECT, SUBJECT AND METHODOLOGY OF THE STUDY

The main objective of the study is to develop the historical-evolutionary approach revealing the regularities of human development in natural evolution, the history of society and construction of individual life course of personality on the basis of the methodology of the systems approach to human development and of the experience of studying personality development in different approaches in psychology.

The object of the study, in line with the objective indicated above, is human development in nature and society, as analyzed in methodological and theoretical approaches in the psychology of personality, established in psychological science.

The *subject of the given study* is the psychology of personality as the history of development of the changing person in a changing world. In a sense, this characteristic of the subject of the psychology of personality in the framework of the historical-evolutionary approach looks like a periphrasis of P.P. Blonsky's saying that behavior can be understood only as history of behavior.

Methodology of the study. The research strategy in the course of the development of the historical-evolutionary approach to the psychology of personality developed with allowance for the capacities of different levels of methodology: philosophical, general scientific, particular scientific, the one of methods and techniques of study (E.G. Yudin). These levels allow us to see the picture of human development in quite different temporary scales - from macroevolution of nature up to the dynamics of decision-making in a concrete life situation. This is why we list from the wide spectrum of the conceptions of human development first of all the ones which determined the general methodological frame and meaning of the historical-evolutionary approach in psychology:

> The conception of the human being as "the human world", produced in the course of the natural-historical process of the development of humankind (K. Marx);
> The criticism of the ideal of rationality in various theories of knowledge (M.K. Mamardashvili);
> The theory of transition of the biosphere into the noosphere (V.I. Vernadsky);
> The conception of behavior of unstable systems in inorganic and living nature (I. Prigogine);
> The synthetic theory of evolution (I.I. Shmalghausen);
> The conception of evolutionary progress (A.N. Severtsov, K.M. Zavadsky);
> The idea of preadaptation in the evolutionary process (N.I. Vavilov);
> The conception of the evolution of goal-directed activity in the framework of the "physiology of activity " (N.A. Bernstein);
> The hypothesis about the role of disseminating selection in anthroposociogenesis (V.P. Alekseev);
> The semiotic conception of culture (Yu.M. Lotman);
> The cultural-historical conception of the development of higher mental functions (L.S. Vygotsky);
> The activity theory approach in psychology (A.N. Leontiev, S.L. Rubinstein).

Besides the methodological sets indicated above, an essential role in the development of the historical-evolutionary approach to the psychology of personality was also played by the concept of carnival culture (M.M. Bakhtin), general psychological theory of set (D.N. Uznadze), the conception of human science (B.G. Ananyev) and the etogenic approach to social behavior (R. Harre).

THE TASKS OF THE STUDY

In line with the main objective, subject and methodology of the study, described above, in this work the following theoretical, practical and social tasks are singled out:

1. Critical analysis of methodological sets of scientific thinking and sociocultural ideological sets of the society that prevent the construction of the subject of the psychology of personality as the developmental history of the changing person in the changing world.
2. Elaboration of the historical-evolutionary approach that removes the barriers on the way of construing the subject of the psychology of personality and opens possibilities for the interdisciplinary synthesis of ideas on personality development in biogenesis, sociogenesis and persogenesis.
3. Singling out the basic principles of activity theory approach to the analysis of transformations of individual-related properties and social-historical way of life in the construction of life course of personality.
4. Revealing the units of analysis of personality structure in the framework of the historical-evolutionary approach in the psychology of personality.
5. Substantiation of the views on education as the sociogenetic mechanism of personality development from the positions of the historical-evolutionary approach.
6. Organization of the psychological service for education as the condition for designing the system of variable education which ensures the extension of possibilities for personality development.

CHAPTER 1

THROUGH THE BARRIERS OF CLASSICAL RATIONAL THINKING

Our study showed that the sources of numerous barriers in the way of construing the psychology of personality are connected, first of all, with overconscious sets, mental schematisms and stereotypes of thinking inherent in classical philosophy and science at the end of XIXth - beginning of XXth century.

Recalling the words of N.N. Lange, who compared a psychologist at the end of XIXth century to Priam on the ruins of Troy, it would be pertinent to continue this capacious analogy and to call the "ideal of rationality" (M.K. Mamardashvili) the Trojan horse that classical philosophy and physics presented to the psychology of XXth century.

In the history of attempts to overcome the consequences of borrowing the schemes of scientific analysis from classical physics, the following milestones are to be indicated:

Revealing the phenomena, the way of setting up problems and general views on human beings, stemming from the research design in line with the canons of rationality ideal;

Reflection of methodological premises and postulates in psychology embodying and laying bare for the psychologists the limitations of classical rational thinking;

Distinguishing psychological approaches and conceptions, containing potentialities for non-classical thinking.

PHENOMENA, LOGICAL DICHOTOMIES AND HUMAN IMAGES

PHENOMENA

In a psychology that designed its research analogously to classical physics, the facts, evidencing the subject's activity, were interpreted as "errors", artifacts or annoying deviations from the norm. As examples one can mention the errors of "expectation" and "habituation" in psychophysical experiments aimed at sensory threshold measurement; "error of stimulus" (E. Titchener), etc. Essentially all the long way of sensory thresholds measurement passed by psychophysics, was the way of struggle with these "errors". This struggle was consecrated by the striving to comprehend typical laws of sensory processes cleared from any influence of the subject's activity - its motivation, sets and, finally, activity itself in which sensory or perceptive processes are included (see [10]). The field of phenomena not falling into the schemes of classical rational thinking and the model of rational adaptive action (M.K. Mamardashvili), following from this scheme, is extremely wide in psychology and related humanitarian sciences. It spreads from the above mentioned "errors" in experimental psychology to deviations from the social or clinical norm, being considered as illogical thinking, primitive consciousness in other cultures, and various strange behavior of the type of "madness" of Czar Paul I, etc. A model of rational predictable adaptable activity, the objectives of which are always represented, transparent and intelligible, strives to rationalize, in the psychoanalytic sense of the word, all the unpredictable, unique, unlike, non-utilitarian. And it is not so important at this point, whether that untypical and unique phenomenon be called, for example, "genius" or "madness". We shall note, following M.K. Mamardashvili, that human history, sifted through the filter of the ideal of rationality, gets rid of all the non-utilitarian, i.e., of all that is believed to be useless, for example, of works of primitive art that cannot be recognized by the archaeologists busy with excavations of understandable and utilitarian tools of labor.

HUMAN IMAGES

The model of rational adaptive activity has also largely defined the "human images", which corresponded to the canons of classical rational thinking. If to roughen the description of "human images", existing in different forms in human sciences, it becomes then possible to distinguish three competing images as follows:

> "a feeling creature" (a recent projection of this image fortified its positions in cognitive psychology as a computer metaphor "human being as an information-processing system");
>
> "a programmed creature" (in behavioral sciences - "human being as a set of responses"; in social sciences - "human being as a repertoire of social roles or scripts");
>
> "a needing creature" ("human being as a collection of needs, drives and motives").

These "human images" corresponded to the model of rational activity. And even treating human drives and motives as "unconscious" did not change the matter, because in psychoanalysis the essential characteristic of rational activity - its subordination to the final, preset goal remains inviolable.

LOGICAL DICHOTOMIES

In quite different approaches and theories in the psychology of personality, some "eternal" questions emerge with amazing persistence, having the form of logical dichotomies representing characteristic signs of rational classical thinking. Here are some examples of most typical questions of this kind: Is human being a biological and/or a social creature? Is a human nature determined by the environment and/or heredity? Is a person a rational and/or an irrational creature? Is human behavior controlled by the program installed from outside or the program of behavior is created by the person every time anew? Is personality structure static or dynamic? What type of adaptation to the environment - passive (reactive) or active - is characteristic of human behavior? Was ancient Greek a personality or not? Behind these questions a view on person as a "thing among things" appears, which, even if placed in the center of universe, is spun-off by the environment, programmed by heredity, and directed by the soul or controlled by the interaction of these three "factors". Investigating such mechanics of "personal bodies" being a hidden analogy of the mechanics of celestial bodies in Newton's classical physical picture of the world, the psychologists get caught in the traps of logical dichotomies and try to give exact answers to questions posed in the style of classical rational thinking.

When the phenomena which do not fall into the schemes of rational adaptive activity and unsolved questions reach some critical point, the psychology addresses the methodology of science and breaks through the barriers of classical rational thinking.

POSTULATES AND METHODOLOGICAL PREMISES OF CLASSICAL RATIONAL THINKING IN PSYCHOLOGY

The classical rational thinking seems "natural" as long as it does not become an object of intense reflection. Just the reflection of postulates and premises of classical thinking is a step to the transformation of culture of thinking, to its "potential relativization" (S.S. Averintsev), rather than to the simple detection of methodological errors. The products of reflection transforming classical rational thinking were conceived as "the postulate of immediacy", "the postulate of compliance", different forms of cognitive egocentrism ("eurocentrism", "lingvocentrism", "evolutionary snobbery", "anthropocentrism"), and some methodological premises of dualistic schemes of determination of personality development.

POSTULATE OF IMMEDIACY

In traditional psychology, the accumulated new facts about, in particular, the manifestations of human activity, unconscious drives, entered into conflict with the *postulate of immediacy*. According to this postulate, objective reality directly influences the human mind and directly determines the subsequent mental and behavioral phenomena. The postulate of immediacy was introduced by D.N. Uznadze when he analyzed the introspective psychology of consciousness and behaviorism. The basis for the postulate of immediacy is formed by the dual scheme of the analysis of mental phenomena inherent in mechanistic determinism: influence at the subject's receptive systems -

subjective or objective responses aroused by it. The most clear expression of the postulate of immediacy was the central scheme of behaviorism "stimulus - response". The acceptance of this postulate results in the position that the subject's activity either falls out of the psychologists' view or is explained by the interference of special subjective factors, different manifestations of the mysterious personality.

The postulate of immediacy represented an overconscious set of thinking, quite typical for thinking in the natural sciences, in particular, in classical physics and traditional physiology. Recognition of the scheme of mechanistic determinism - the postulate of immediacy - produced an isolation of psychological reality from life by the representatives of traditional psychology, oriented in their research to the experiences of a separate individual or to the facts of behavior, who found themselves either in a closed circle of consciousness or in a closed circle of behavior. In both cases the human being was separated from the world. As a result, various closed "worlds" became the subject of psychological research: "mind without behavior" and "behavior without mind". In domestic psychology the postulate of immediacy is overcome in D.N. Uznadze's theory of set and in the activity theory approach to studying mental phenomena (see [1], [5], [52]).

ANTHROPOCENTRISM (ANTHROPOCENTRIC PARADIGM OF THINKING)

The essence of a human being is supposed to be either in itself or in the environment (biological, social or physical) influencing him/her. The problem of relations between the biological and the social is elaborated in the context of a biologized, sociologized or psychologized *anthropocentric paradigm* of thinking about the human being in terms of "person without world" and "world without person". In other words, a dualistic view of the human being that follows from the anthropocentric paradigm of thinking extracts the person from nature and society and then, applying the schemes of two-factor determination of human development, transforms the human being into a centaur from ancient Greek myths - half-animal, half-human, half-biological and half-social creature.

ABSOLUTIZATION OF PHYLOGENETIC, SOCIOGENETIC, ONTOGENETIC REGULARITIES OF HUMAN DEVELOPMENT

The anthropocentric paradigm of thinking about the human being often leads to the view of a human being outside the history of human development or to the absolutization of regularities of some stage of the natural-historical process of human evolution.

Stormy discussions about the "degree of animality" or "degree of humanness" of the human being, as a rule, begin with an analysis of the "biosocial" nature of human being in ontogenesis or make a record leap in time from phylogenesis to ontogenesis. The changes of human being in course of evolution of his way of life in anthropogenesis and sociogenesis are thereby excluded from consideration.

The human being is a social-genetic creature not only because he or she is born into society. His/her birth is based on a highly intricate process of transformation of evolutionary regularities of a way of life in the history of phylogenesis, anthropogenesis and sociogenesis.

In this regard, the question of the "degree of animality" and "degree of sociality" of the human being in the society is incorrect from the very outset. This, firstly, separates the person from the society in which he or she lives; secondly, it abstracts from the history of transformation of the way of life of the human species in anthropogenesis and sociogenesis, ignores the specificity of history of the human species in evolution, as well as the change in regularities of this evolution.

An example of such a leap from phylogenesis and embryogenesis to the field of typology of personality is W. Sheldon's constitutional theory of personality. W. Sheldon takes the concept of "somatotype" (type of bodily constitution) as the basis of his theory. From three layers of embryonic leafs in embryogenesis he extracts three different somatotypes. Then, from them he arrives at temperament types, personality's character, and then to the regularities of social development. The regularities of embryogenesis, common for different biological species in phylogenesis, are considered absolute and treated as regularities of social development. W. Sheldon's conception not only misses the social origins of personality. In a still greater degree than the behaviorism, it immerses the process of human development into the deepest layers of biological evolution, thus forgetting the specificity of Homo Sapiens.

An example of the absolutization of sociogenetic regularities and their direct projection onto the ontogenesis of personality is S. Holl's conception of recapitulation, which establishes the relations of isomorphism between three different periods of human development - embryogenesis, sociogenesis and ontogenesis. According to Hall, a child in his/her individual development reproduces all the phases of the development of society (animal phase, phase of hunting and fishing, end of wildness and the beginning of civilization, etc.), as the embryo passes the main stages of phylogenesis.

Behind these examples we find the absolutization of particular real regularities of the evolutionary process and the isolation of the process of personality development from anthropogenetic, sociogenetic and ontogenetic natural-historical process of human development. Personality development is mediated by the history of anthropogenesis and sociogenesis of the human species, and therefore the issue of the existence of the animal, "inferior" instance in humans etc. misses the fact that the human being is born human in the human world.

"UNILINEAR" EVOLUTIONISM

In positivistically based psychology, the processes of development have been often interpreted in terms of "unilinear" evolutionism. As a result, psychology, first, found itself under the power of linear schemes of development, dissecting developmental processes into "stages", "periods", "phases" of anthropogenesis, sociogenesis, ontogenesis or information processing "blocks" in the actual genesis of the mental image, mechanically combined with each other. Second, following the logic of linear evolutionism, psychology ordered the stages of human development according to the principle "the earlier, the more primitive, the later, the more complicated, more developed". The stereotype of the "unilinear" evolutionism turned into a kind of "evolutionary snobbery" and resulted in the following conclusions: visual thinking is more primitive than logical thinking; the "artistic type" (I.P. Pavlov) is lower than "thinking type"; unconscious manifestations in child development like as in the autistic character of thinking, weakness of introspection, non-sensitivity to the contradictions is rougher, more archaic, "underdeveloped" as compared to consciousness. The absurdity of "unilinear" evolutionism becomes obvious when one addresses the history of culture and concludes that Iliya Repin stays at a lower and more primitive level than Iliya Glazunov just because the former was born, to his misfortune, in the "lower" ninetieth century rather that in "highly civilized" twentieth century. In fact, cultures and psychologies of previous generations are not at all simpler, more primitive, rougher or lower. They are just *different,* construed by different views that can, however, provide a full-weight adaptive effect in evolution. The idea of the *heterogeneity of thinking* (L. Levy-Bruhl) is helpful in overcoming the unilinear evolutionism by the study of sociogenesis and persogenesis. This idea of heterogeneity of thinking, that makes it possible to understand the coexistence of both pralogical and logical thinking in the mind of a person, belonging to a certain culture, has been elaborated in the framework of cultural-historical psychology by P. Tuliviste. Further development of this statement leads to the idea of the historical heterogeneity of personality and, thereby, points at another direction of movement above the barriers of classical rational thinking (see [3], [5], [29]).

EUROCENTRISM

Such a typical egocentric stereotype of thinking as "eurocentrism" also hinders the study of sociogenetic and persogenetic regularities of personality development. Many cross-cultural studies suffer from eurocentrism, taking the examples of treating personality, regularities of its functioning and development in European culture as something absolute, given once and forever, and then taking these examples as the only reference system while studying the personality in other cultures and civilizations. As a result, for example, eurocentrism naturalizes the logic of European thinking and assigns it the status of "natural" characteristic of thinking, similar to the color of eyes or hair. In fact, formal logic is just a cultural-historical invention, that is, it is *set* by the culture rather than *granted* to us. In this connection it would be reasonable to assume the possibility of invention and existence of other logics; the formal logic would thus take an appropriate place among different coexisting reference systems (see [5], [29]).

LINGVOCENTRISM

In an extensive cycle of research of different aspects of personal communication, lingvocentrism is dominant, that is *describing the regularities of any communication upon a model of verbal communication*. As a result, the biblical saying "in the beginning was the Word" in many aspects defines the logic of research in behavioral and social sciences, including the understanding of the objective world as materialization of symbolical activity (L. von Bertalanfi), as well as underlies a new image of the human being as a rational "symbolical creature", a "linguistic person", etc. Lingvocentrism finds its extreme manifestation in the hypothesis of "linguistic determinism" (E. Super). The vulnerability of the lingvocentric set appeared by studying nonverbal semiotic systems. It mixes phylogenetic, sociogenetic and ontogenetic aspects of nonverbal communications. The limitation of lingvocentrism became especially evident in numerous attempts to create a discrete alphabet of nonverbal communications language. The impossibility to embody the simultaneous sense manifestations of personality in discrete indifferent signs dooms beforehand to failure any search for discrete formalized lexicons of gestures and body movements and by that proves the necessity to transcend the borders of the lingvocentrism in modern psychology of personality (see [44], [72]).

THE "ARTIFICIAL WORLDS" INSTEAD OF THE "HUMAN WORLD IN THE NATURAL-HISTORICAL PROCESS"

The paradoxicality of different views on "environment", "culture", etc. becomes evident because these so-called "environments", for example, "the physical environment" in I. Newton's theory, Euclidean "geometrical space", Descarte's "coordinate system" are human inventions, as well as any other system manifestations of the material world. In psychology, many efforts were undertaken to place the person into the "world of raw experience". The logic of such research in psychology was regularly criticized for the artificiality of the analysis procedures, for placing the person in unusual conditions. It has been, however, missed that the "world of raw experience" is not the physical habitat of human being, but rather the reality discovered by actual science and considered as the "physical environment". Hypertrophy of "culture", in turn, resulted in the concept that the environment influencing human development was reduced to the "world of impersonal social norms" which, as ready-made clothes, are put on the biological figure of the individual. From the real facts of the existence of social norms in the "human world", the researcher, influenced by two-factor determination schemes of personality development, is compelled to conclude about the existence of two isolated worlds - the "world of social norms", inherent in some typical person in the given culture, and "psychophysiological world" of the individual, whose natural individual peculiarities somewhat determine the adjustment to these social norms (R. Linton).

In analyzing "artificial worlds" subordinated to the inviolable laws of classical science, there comes an amazing impression that many researchers in the psychology of personality try at any price to put the study of personality into the frame of depersonalized rational science, while some modern chemists and mathematicians, like I. Prigogine, N.N. Moiseyev, rose against the dehumanized world of Newtonian rationality. The clock was frequently used as the symbol of rationality of the world order. I. Prigogine showed that the rationality-based views of the world as an automatic one and on the world as a God-ruled one, converge: automate needs God. It is the acceptance of a rational mechanistic picture of nature and society, the picture of a world of universal laws of balance and order, draws together the characteristics of the "artificial worlds" in which any individual manifestations of human life are subordinated to the homeostasis principle.

POSTULATE OF COMPLIANCE

The "postulate of compliance" (V.A. Petrovsky) underlies various directions in psychological theory and methodology explicitly or implicitly expressing the sets of classical rational thinking. In the context of this postulate, any manifestation of the subject's activity is considered as moving toward a preset final Goal, to which the whole life course of the personality is finally subordinated. The subordination of activity to any given norm or goal makes the essential feature of the subject's behavior labeled as an adaptive one. V.A. Petrovsky distinguished three variants of the postulate of compliance: homeostatic, hedonistic and pragmatic, based on the character of the preset goal.

HOMEOSTATIC VARIANT

The idea of homeostasis was inherited by psychologists from traditional biological theories, stating that all the responses of an organism as a system, passively adjusting to the environmental influences, are only to fulfil a special adaptive function, namely, to bring the organism back to a state of equilibrium. In empirical psychology this variant took many different forms. Especially explicitly it appeared in reflexology, where the subject's activity was reduced to maintaining a balance with the environment. The homeostatic variant of the explanation of a person's behavior found its expression in such unlike general psychological theories as S. Freud's psychoanalysis; K. Lewin's dynamic theory of personality; social-psychological theories of discharging cognitive dissonance (L. Festinger) or achieve cognitive balance (Ch. Osgood and others); neobehavioristic theories of the reduction of tension of organic needs in humans and animals. In the historical-evolutionary approach it is shown that the conceptions of personality in humanistic psychology is just seemingly different but basically close. In these conceptions the idea of "striving to maintain tension", to break the balance is opposed to the idea of homeostasis, appearing as a basic methodological premise for the study of motivation of personality development (A. Maslow, G. Allport, C. Rogers and others). In both cases the person is opposed to social environment, and its behavior is subordinated to a preset ultimate goal - either to find a balance with society by means of needs discharge, or to reach the balance with oneself by the way of self-actualization, i.e., to become as prescribed by nature, irrespective whether society hinders or helps it.

HEDONISTIC VARIANT

According to the hedonistic premise of the human behavior analysis, any behavioral acts are aimed at the maximization of pleasure and minimization of suffering, particularly negative emotions, afflictions, etc.

PRAGMATIC VARIANT

This variant, widespread in functional and cognitive psychology, states that any optimal behavior is aimed at maximal benefit or useful effect by minimal efforts. The pragmatic variant, especially in the form it takes in cognitive psychology, is based on the definition of the human being as a "reasonable and rational being" and considers any human action as rational and reasonable. Hence in the analysis of the development of a person in its individual life and in the history of society, all the manifestations that don't fit into the frame of "reasonable action" - unmotivated acts in a person's life, nonutilitarian manifestations of a person in the history of society - are discarded.

Psychologists, anthropologists and archaeologists seek explanations for manifestations of the essence of personality in its individual life and in the history of mankind in purely rational adaptive formations - in the utilitarian useful activity and its products. Here the image of "reasonable creature", corresponding to the pragmatic variant of the postulate of compliance, is completed and proved, while many nonutilitarian manifestations in the life of a person and mankind are interpreted as negligible, strange, unnecessary and useless.

Among the three mentioned variants of the postulate of compliance, the *homeostatic model of development* influenced the understanding of personality development in the context of biogenetic, sociogenetic and persogenetic orientations in psychology most of all. It is the homeostatic model, reducing any manifestations of activity in the course of evolution to achieving an equilibrium, which underlies the schemes of two-factor determination of personality development. The homeostatic model forms the basis for such different developmental theories as S. Freud's psychoanalysis and J. Piaget's genetic psychology. At the same time, various phenomena analyzed by V.S. Rotenberg in psychosomatics, and by V.A. Petrovsky in the psychology of a person's activity, prove that the homeostatic model of development is not universal, but rather special. For instance, among the facts not complying with this model there are the facts of a decrease of psychosomatic and infectious diseases in extreme and critical situations, "the illness of goal achievement, Martin Eden's syndrome" (V.S. Rotenberg), and such phenomenon as "risk for risk's sake" (V.A. Petrovsky). These facts urge psychologists not only to shift to "another side of the postulate of compliance", as was precisely indicated by V.A. Petrovsky in his book "The Person in Psychology" (1996), the spirit of which is congenial to works in non-classical physics, but also to break through the above barriers of classical rational thinking in the psychology of personality.

CHAPTER 2

FROM THE CULTURE OF USEFULNESS - TO THE CULTURE OF DIGNITY: SOCIAL BIOGRAPHY OF CULTURAL-HISTORICAL PSYCHOLOGY

The sources of non-classical thinking in the psychology of personality are closely connected with the development of the problem of the unconscious in psychoanalysis (S. Freud), with the theory of set (D.N. Uznadze), with the cultural-historical theory of the development of higher mental functions (L.S. Vygotsky) and the activity theory approach to the study of mental phenomena (A.N. Leontiev, S.L. Rubinstein; see [1]; [22]; [29]; [34]; [55]; [66]).

The essential novelty of these various directions in the methodology of psychology is the breakthrough beyond the "postulate of immediacy" and search of a "mediating link" which would generate mental phenomena, without belonging to the mental sphere itself. In psychoanalysis, the emphasis on such features of the unconscious as "non-sensitivity to contradictions" and "timelessness" caused fear and disgust in the representatives of classical rational thinking which hastened to rationalize psychoanalysis as "not a science", "mythology" or strange "art". The D.N. Uznadze's theory of set from the very beginning protested against the rational image of a human being as an isolated creature, pulled out from the world of evolution. A supergoal for D.N. Uznadze was the study of the human being as an active creator of the "biosphere" (the term was introduced by D.N. Uznadze in 1923 independently from V.I. Vernadsky). Therefore the ideas of goal determination of life activity and "functional tendencies" of personality as the source for self-movement of activity were inherent in D.N. Uznadze's methodology from the first stages of the development of the theory of primary set.

Special attention in the development of the historical-evolutionary approach to the psychology of personality was given to those ideological value sets of public consciousness which pushed out of psychological science the non-classical paradigm of thinking in psychology, underlying cultural-historical psychology and the activity theory approach to studying mental phenomena, for years.

Only in the last decades have the names of L.S. Vygotsky, A.N. Leontiev, S.L. Rubinstein become more often associated with the shaping of the non-classical thinking paradigm in psychological science. Among L.S. Vygotsky's followers, D.B. Elkonin (1981) was the one who directly characterized Vygotsky's ideas as a non-classical approach to consciousness. As a matter of fact, the myth about L.S. Vygotsky as a rationalist, spiritually close to cognitive psychology or even to neobehaviorism, begins to break down in the West thanks to works of R. Harre, J. Wertsch, M. Cole and a group of Danish methodologists of psychology (H. Poulsen, N. Engelstedt, J. Mammen and others, 1988) who unambiguously showed the connections between the profound premises of the activity theory approach in psychology and N. Bohr's non-classical physics.

In his revolt against rationalism, P. Harre (1984, 1985) involves L.S. Vygotsky as an ally and, based on the principle of "interiorization-exteriorization", takes two steps:

he accuses classical psychology of five sins - scientism, universalism, individualism, mechanistic causality and basing upon Cartesian oppositions "external - internal", "subjective - objective";

he builds a space for "true" psychology with three basic axes: "individual - collective", "social - personal", "public - private" with a direct reference to L.S. Vygotsky's idea of "interiorization-exteriorization".

The above-mentioned Danish psychologists discover in the activity theory approach the methodology that removes the opposition "objective - subjective" through the category of activity and, in fact, uses the "complementarily principle" (N. Bohr) in the analysis of relationships between the physical, cultural and mental world.

For D.B. Elkonin, L.S. Vygotsky's transition from an interpretation of social environment as a "factor" to the understanding of the "social" as the *"source"* of personality development symbolizes the beginning of the *non-classical psychology of consciousness*.

And it is the strength of L.S. Vygotsky's cultural-historical psychology rather than its weakness that this theory is often perceived as closer by spirit to art than to psychology based on classical rational thinking.

The secret of L.S. Vygotsky's contemporaneity in the history of science was nearly found by S. Toulmin, A. Puzyrei, A. Kozulin who, while speaking about "the phenomenon of Vygotsky" as a riddle of twentieth century, come very close to its solution in their characteristics of L.S. Vygotsky. S. Freud taught us that metaphors have a hidden meaning. These authors compared Vygotsky with Mozart, and his fate with the fates of literary characters by M.Cervantes, T. Mann, H. Hesse and B. Pasternak, thus presenting a key to the understanding of the "phenomenon of Vygotsky" and his special path in science. Vygotsky always, even when his texts were clothed in behavioristic or reflexological scientific terminology, maintained the profound position of Master, genuine artist concerned with the construction of cultural concrete human psychology. Cultural-historical psychology thus became a product of a new culture of understanding the human being, generated in the creative workshops of L.S. Vygotsky and his companions. In terms of the poetic typology of Osip Mandelshtam, so much appreciated by Vygotsky himself, one can say that Vygotsky was the "meaning-seeker" rather than "rational formalist".

It is true, that the ideas of Vygotsky's school have been later put, as some philosophers note, into an anabiosis for years. But this was so not at all because these ideas dealt with the spheres of logic, philosophy or culturology, and psychologists had not understood their significance. The cause of the delay in the development of cultural-historical theory, its slowing down and dividing into many outflows from the main channel, that sometimes seem not connected to each other, lays in the social history of society rather than in science itself.

In order to understand the social biography of cultural-historical psychology, it is necessary first of all to place the mosaic of cultures through human history at two poles - the pole of *usefulness* and the pole of *dignity*. *In the culture of usefulness* the idea that the universe is like a huge clock started by a wise watch-maker prevails. Everything is measured, predictable and subordinated to the order of social activities given once and forever. In fiction such a rational social world was precisely depicted in the utopias "We" by E. Zamyatin and "1984" by G. Orwell. But, as was sung in a Soviet song - "we're born to make a tale come true". Utopias of E. Zamyatin and G. Orwell have come true, become embodied in the impersonal culture of usefulness. Any concrete human psychology and, to be sure, humanistic cultural-historical psychology was alien to the essence of this culture. By the fact of their existence they threatened the foundations of this culture and thereby were dangerous and excessive for it.

The culture of usefulness is "equipped" with the sort of ideological filters which sensitively determine which "human image" has a right to exist in mentality and society, be a subject of scientific research. The image of "marionette person", "behavioral robot", even if it was not realized by researchers, was mostly justified by works in the field of conditioned reflexes, reflexology and reactology. It was just this image of "reflexological robot" that was finally demanded by the command-administrative system of totalitarian socialism.

In the 1930's a shadow of the totalitarian socialist culture of usefulness slowly but consistently crawled into genetics, the philosophy of the noosphere and pedagogy. Alongside with genetics and philosophy preaching the "principle of solidarity", even human science was ostracized.

Vygotsky's school of cultural-historical psychology had been rapidly forming in those years as practical developmental psychology, the basis of pedology - science of child development and education. But the command-administrative system built in 1930s did not need psychological research for the development of individuality, assessment of individual abilities in children. It was a time when in the atmosphere of total unification barrack-like pedagogy began to affirm. The program of cultural-historical psychology clearly diverged then with the program of building a totalitarian socialism.

The culture of usefulness claimed to have the exclusive right to decide where a person should go, where to be, what to think about. A sharp contrast to the imperatives of culture of usefulness were the letters written by L.S. Vygotsky in 1930 and 1931: "Every person must know where he/she is. You and me - we also know it and must stand firmly. Therefore the result: you, rather than someone else, should write about the reaction of choice, this chapter about the developing human freedom from external constraints of things and their will...". "...It is impossible to live without conceiving life spiritually. Without philosophy (own, personal, living) there may be nihilism, cynicism, suicide, but not life. But everybody has one's own philosophy. It is necessary to grow it in oneself, because it supports life in us.... What can shake a person seeking truth? How much inner light, heat, support is in this seeking and striving! And the most important is the life itself - sky, sun, love, people, suffering. This is real, not just words. This is genuine. This is interwoven in life. Crises are not temporary states, but a path of inner life. When we pass from systems to fates.... birth and death of systems, we will see this ourselves". ("It is impossible to live not conceiving life spiritually": L.S. Vygotsky's letters to his disciples and colleagues. Published by A. Puzyrei, Znanie - Sila, 1990, N 7, p. 93-94). To comment on these lines, their amazing irrelevance and absurdity in 1930's, would be like retelling poetry in prose. This is enough to feel the drama of both L.S. Vygotsky's fate and the fate of a whole program of cultural-historical psychology.

The culture of usefulness does not need people and sciences oriented to personal fate, to that what underlies each person - capacity to change, variability, unpredictability. Such sciences, be it Vygotsky's cultural-historical psychology, Vernadsky's noosphere theory or Vavilov's genetics, are dangerous for the totalitarian system, because they assert the right for unpredictability, variability in the society. By that, they call into question the basic model of a transparent world which can be handled by an all-seeing watchmaker according to a plan.

The followers of Vygotsky after his death somehow stepped back to the territory of "partial" activities such as memory, perception, thinking. Discussions about these processes as higher forms of behavior have temporarily faded. Nevertheless, even in research at the end of 1930's, the position prevailed that can be expressed by the brief formula - "In the beginning was a deed" (L.S. Vygotsky). The ideas of cultural-historical psychology which has been forced underground were demanded again in the years of the Second World War, when scholastic labels and ideological speculations became out of date. In A.R. Luria's research on the restoration of brain functions following damage a new science - neuropsychology – arose. The psychology for motivation of behavior and higher forms of voluntary behavior was developed in a series of works by A.N. Leontiev and A.V. Zaporozhets, summarized in their still contemporary book "Rehabilitation of hand function" (1945). N.A. Bernstein, in a classic of modern human science, continues his dialogue with Vygotsky, vigorously discussing with A.N.

Leontiev, A.R. Luria and A.V. Zaporozhets the results of research on movement construction. Like L.S. Vygotsky, N.A. Bernstein welcomes a protest against the image of "human marionette" clearly seen in works by A.R. Luria, A.N. Leontiev and A.V. Zaporozhets. However, the command-administrative system was only temporarily forgetting "reservations" whereas the ideas of cultural-historical psychology, activity theory approach to studying mental phenomena and physiology of activity survived. The image of "human marionette", acting on by pressing a button, became again firmly established in science after the sad and well-known Pavlovian session in 1950.

Enlightenment came after Stalin's death in 1953, in the epoch of Khrushchev's thaw. In 1957, as French psychologist R. Zazzo evidences, A.N. Leontiev when in France told his colleagues A. Wallon and R. Zazzo that "Pavlovian psychology" was becoming history and strongly recommended publishing the works by L.S. Vygotsky then poorly known abroad. Unfortunately, this attempt of A.N. Leontiev was not a success. L.S. Vygotsky's "Selected psychological essays" with a foreword by A.N. Leontiev and A.R. Luria, appeared only in 1956 in the USSR.

By the beginning of the 1970's, cultural-historical psychology, having experienced the tragedy of being unclaimed for years, started again to sprout in the research of V.V. Davydov, V.P. Zinchenko, A.V. Petrovsky, O.K. Tikhomirov and other followers of Vygotsky, Leontiev and Luria. However, *the problem of mechanisms transforming culture into the world of personality, and especially the problem of generating another culture in the course of personality development still remains on the roadside of the social biography of cultural-historical psychology.*

One who is immersed in the innermost depths of cultural-historical psychology passes both explicitly and implicitly from the analysis of "consciousness outside culture" and "culture outside consciousness" to the comprehension of the secret of transitions, transformations of social relations into person's world and creating the worlds of human culture from the material of these relations by the personality. *To realize the original project of cultural-historical psychology means to see it as the discipline which crowns the knowledge of human development in nature and society, aiming at understanding the mechanisms of transformation of culture into the world of personality and generation of culture during personality development.*

Cultural-historical psychology was able to establish this problem because (as has been recently stated by D.B. Elkonin, R. Harre and others) it was in methodological aspects a transition from the classical rational thinking to the non-classical style of thinking; and in the axiological aspect it was a moral imperative, upholding the necessity of the shift from the culture of usefulness to the culture of dignity.

In this research it is specially emphasized that by the style of thinking, cultural-historical psychology is closer to art than to rational science. In this respect the words of O.E. Mandelshtam that literary schools live not only by ideas, but also by tastes are applicable to the L.S. Vygotsky's school. Thanks to L.S. Vygotsky's school, *a new taste* has arisen and the cultural space of psychology has opened still wider for sociologists (E. Durkheim, G. Mead), ethnographers (L. Levy-Bruhl, F. Boas, R. Turnvald), linguists (F. de Saussure, A.A. Potebnya, R. Jakobson), biologists (V.A. Wagner, A.N. Severtsov). Just as the best writers have grown up from Gogol's "Overcoat", it is from the L.S. Vygotsky's school, with its tendency to break the disciplinary boundaries, that neuropsychology and neurolinguistics (A.R. Luria), psycholinguistics (A.A. Leontiev), psychosemantics (V.F. Petrenko, A.G. Shmelev), psychopedagogy in the broad sense of the word (P.Ya. Galperin, D.B. Elkonin, V.V. Davydov, N.F. Talyzina), psychodidactics (L.V. Zankov), socio-historical approach to the education, cultural psychology and pedagogy of the "dialogue of cultures" (J. Wertsch, M. Cole, V.S. Bibler) have grown up.

Just as a coiled spring, L.S. Vygotsky's pedological program straightened out and started to work in the educational system beginning in 1988, being realized in such a constructive discipline as the psychology of education. The above-mentioned of works of R. Harre, Danish and other psychologists also proves that not only manuscripts, but also the tastes and ideas of non-classical psychology do not burn even in the fires of the culture of usefulness. At last, it was the taste of L.S. Vygotsky's school to the systems historical-genetic analysis of human development in the evolution of nature and history of culture that led to the development of the historical-evolutionary approach in the psychology of personality.

CHAPTER 3

GENERAL SYSTEM PRINCIPLES IN AN ANALYSIS OF HUMAN DEVELOPMENT WITH THE HISTORICAL-EVOLUTIONARY APPROACH

The author believes that the systems-historical methodology makes it possible to discover new facets of the human image in different systems and results in the formulation of general systems principles of the analysis of the - human being in the evolution of nature and society ([4]; [5]; [6]; [27]; [33]; [34]; [35]; [64]; [77]).

Studying systems aspects of human development in the historical-evolutionary approach takes into account phenomena and regularities revealed in history, sociology, semiology, and evolutionary biology. The reason for referring to these seemingly unconnected sciences is that general systems regularities have been discovered in them. One of the functions for general scientific systems analysis is that it helps to single out common regularities of systems development from concrete sciences about nature and society thus establishing a communication channel between different human sciences. The necessity of studying the human being in the process of evolution of the system that produces it assumes that the researcher not just speaks about the development, but every time puts the question about the evolutionary meaning of this or that phenomenon in such a system. For example, what is the evolutionary meaning of a new species appearing in biological evolution or different ethnic groups (tribes, nations) in the history of humankind; what is the evolutionary meaning of new organs appearing in the phylogenesis of a certain species or of a unique character taking shape during the individual life course of a person? Studying developmental regularities of systems (both biological and social ones), the mechanics of their development, would be incomplete unless the evolutionary meaning is discovered, for the sake of which all the developmental mechanics, for example, mechanisms of natural selection (N.A. Bernstein, N.I. Vavilov, A.N. Severtsov, I.I. Shmalgauzen, S.N. Davidenkov), do function.

The systems analysis of development thereby states the *necessity of studying the human phenomenon in the process of evolution of the system generating it* and of studying the *goal determination* of the developing system. This assumes the question *"For what"* does the phenomenon appear, besides the questions "How does the phenomenon occur?" and "Why it occurs?" (N.A. Bernstein), typical for traditional natural science.

A systems-oriented methodology of human science is based on the statement that the key to understanding human nature in those various systems within which he or she lives rather than in the human being itself as a corporal object. In natural sciences this idea was articulated in the most condensed way in V.I. Vernadsky's fundamental studies. He upheld consistently the idea of the necessity of transition from the individual's level of analysis of biological properties of the human being to studying humans in population-specific, biocenotic and biosphere levels of life organization, and social properties of the human being - in the system of the noosphere, the one produced by the creative activity of mankind within the sphere of mind. Both the systems approach principle for the analysis of human nature in the context of the development of various systems and V.I. Vernadsky's ideas try hard to force their way in the minds of representatives of different disciplines, meeting a barrier of the natural view of the human being as an autonomous natural or social object.

In psychology, the necessity of studying human development based on the regularities of the historical-evolutionary process in nature and society was repeatedly mentioned by such researchers as B.G. Ananiev, L.S. Vygotsky, A.N. Leontiev, A.R. Luria, S.L. Rubinstein and D.N. Uznadze. In the physiology of higher nervous activity, the problem of *systemogenesis* of the entire human organism was elaborated by P.K. Anokhin, the author of functional systems theory. Original views on the regularities of personality development in a social group from the viewpoint of the traditional theory of evolution have been formulated by the American psychologist T. Campbell.

In the systems approach to human development, attention is more and more focused on the universal regularities of the evolutionary process, discovered by the scientific school of evolutionary biology of A.N. Severtsov and I.I. Shmalgauzen. Therefore, questions about the criteria of progress for both living and technical self-regulating systems (K.M. Zavadsky, V.I. Varshavsky, D.A. Pospelov), evolutionary regularities of anthroposociogenesis and ethnic communities (V.P. Alekseyev, Y.V. Bromley, G.P. Grigoriev), general mechanisms of cultural evolution (E.S. Markaryan) are raised. An important step on the way to studying general regularities of co-evolution - harmonious mutually conditioning development of nature and society—became the research of V.I. Vernadsky's follower N.N. Moiseyev, summarized in his work "Algorithms of development" (1987).

On the basis of the above-mentioned spectrum of research, a number of principles of the historical-evolutionary approach can be outlined, expressing universal regularities of the development of various systems.

PRINCIPLE 1

The principle of increasing variability of elements of a system as the criterion of progressive evolution: the more advanced the system, the higher the variability of its elements. An outstanding achievement of A.N. Severtsov, a classic of evolutionary biology, was his teaching about two types of progress in evolution: biological and morphophysiological. *Biological* progress consists of *changes in the way of life and position the species occupies in the biosphere; morphophysiological progress means changes in the structure and functions of an animal's body.* Behind this differentiation we find changes in the researchers' thinking about the evolutionary process, the transition from "organism-centered" study of development to the systems vision of the regularities of the evolutionary process. While the vulgar transference of regularities of biological evolution onto the history of society is reasonably criticized, scientists sometimes miss A.N. Severtsov's fundamental discovery. He assumed the possibility of evolution of a way of life, that is the system-making basis of the species' development, relatively independently of the morphophysiological evolution of organisms that prevails in the organic world. The way of life determines the position the species occupies in the biosphere. It determines whether evolution goes the way of *aromorphosis, ideoadaptation or regress.* Under aromorphosis, A.N. Severtsov understood progressive evolution of the way of life leading to the appearance of *new features* in the species, that increase the level of the species' vital activity, enhancing its adaptive capacities which can be useful in case of critical changes in the environment. A.N. Severtsov's idea of *aromorphosis* is similar to N.I. Vavilov's idea of *preadaptations* emerging in the course of evolution, that is, useful features emerging *before* they are really of use for the evolving system. A.N. Severtsov distinguished aromorphosis from ideoadaptation, i.e., adaptation in the narrow sense, as specialization of the species ensuring its best adjustment to its typical living conditions. If evolution goes the way of ideoadaptation, partial adaptations, the species' way of life does not undergo qualitative changes and remains at the same level. Aromorphosis can lead to a new way of life, i.e., entail a change of the system-making basis defining the main characteristics of the given species.

At the level of methodology of the systems approach, the regularities of evolutionary progress described by A.N. Severtsov were summarized and elaborated further in the research of K.M. Zavadsky, V.I. Varshavsky and D.A. Pospelov. It was emphasized in their works that the appearance and the progressive development of any evolving system is provided by the processes of its integration and differentiation - synthesogenesis and segregatiogenesis (K.M. Zavadsky).

According to Zavadsky, integration of elements into a whole, i.e., birth of systems, is not a premise of systems research, but rather a fact requiring explanation. In evolution, the forms living isolated were pressed by numerous forms with collective organization, which in the course of their development took ecological niches one by one. Thereby the whole course of evolutionary process as if experimentally proved the advantages of the group way of life as compared to the isolated one. But this victory raises questions: what is the evolutionary meaning of the synthesogenetic process (integration of separate elements into systems)? What kinds of communities can be considered systems ensuring further development of the species?

Synthesogenesis means integration of separate elements into a system, a set, which opens the possibility of solving problems hitherto insoluble for any of the elements comprising the system. *In synthesogenesis, the number of potentially possible features, which a system might need while facing unforeseen situations, increases.* Synthesogenesis thus explains why the elements should unite into one system in the course of development. By means of synthesogenesis systems are formed ensuring adaptation to a wider range of situations, because their elements have acquired new properties – *the possibilities to interact in order to achieve different goals*, as well as a special resource that can be used in unforeseen circumstances.

In evolution, alongside with synthesogenesis-producing associations able to solve a broad spectrum of tasks, another process of breaking systems into subsystems, i.e., the process of differentiation goes on. Highly specialized subsystems are born capable of fulfilling just one task, but with extreme efficiency. This path of system development leading to specialization was called segregatiogenesis by K.M. Zavadsky. In the evolution of biological, technical and social systems, there are many manifestations of segregatiogenesis as progressive development, ensuring optimum possibilities for a system to solve typical repeated problems. At the same time, specialization of a subsystem, its rigid adaptation to a single class of problems becomes, only if segregatiogenesis is not combined with synthesogenesis, a deadlock for the evolving system and hinders its existence in unforeseen situations. Following the principle of utility, adjusting only to the problems of the present situation, the system developing this way loses advantages achieved by integration of elements into a group, loses the possibility to interact in attaining different goals and disintegrates. Therefore, the evolving system has to find a sort of compromise between superspecialization, which can entail utilitarian path of segregatiogenesis, and universality.

It follows from A.N. Severtsov's theory of changes in the way of life as the basis of progress, from the ideas of synthesogenesis and segregatiogenesis of evolving systems that it is within a system, that an "element" acquires the potential for variativity, manifestation of individual variability. Individual features of an active "element", special and original as they may seem, basically have systems' origin and owe the system even the fact of their existence. In the light of the above considerations, to oppose an "element" to a "system", "individual variativity" to the "species" and "person's individuality" to the "society" seems irrelevant.

These oppositions are consequences of the anthropocentric view of the human being trying to solve the problem. The "what for" personality is then born, which is the necessity of the phenomenon of personality in the historical process of social development, being closed within the space of the organism. Answering this question from the position of traditional psychology, which studies separate individual, his/her cognitive, motivational-emotional and volitional spheres, one considers personality the highest integrating instance controlling mental processes, "the master" of mental functions (W. James). As a result, personality appears in traditional psychology as placed somewhere "above" mental processes, with the main mission to collect these processes into a single bunch of mental functions and to provide them with a certain direction. Such a solution of the issue about the nature of personality places personality both outside mind and outside society.

Such a neglect of the issue of meaning of personality phenomenon in evolution would be justified if the facts about personality, interindividual differences and regularities of the evolutionary process of the development of human species were not absolutely connected. But are the manifestations of variativity in ontogenesis of any organism and the evolution of its species independent things? A quite certain and negative answer to this blunt and naive for any evolutionist question was given by Russian biopsychologist V.A. Wagner.

On the basis of an analysis of relationships between individual and specific mental abilities, first of all individual and specific endowments in different biological species, V.A. Wagner revealed the following regularity: *the higher a community is developed, the moreare manifestations of individuals belonging to the community.* For instance, individual differences in the endowment of the lowest animals living isolated are very small. "For animals living in a herd with a leader where dangers for the members of the herd can be prevented are easier than in case of isolated living, where the role of natural selection becomes less crucial; minor deviations are not eliminated. This results in individual deviations from the specific type of endowment. Despite their insignificance, the fact of their occurrence itself represents the phenomenon of tremendous fundamental significance: here we meet for the first time the phenomena of individual, rather than specific, endowment" (Wagner V.A. *Origin and development of mental abilities.* Issue 7. *Evolution of mental abilities along clean and mixed lines.* Leningrad, 1928. p. 35).

Further V.A. Wagner, comparing fluctuations in individual endowment with the complexity of communities of different species in the process of evolution, showed that these deviations continue to increase, reaching an apogee in human society. From these observations follows the fact of covariation between the variability of mental abilities in individuals and the evolution of species. Thereby the role of individual variability in the extension of evolving systems becomes more obvious.

The increase of individual endowment along with increasing complexity of communities in the process of evolution, as depicted by V.A. Wagner, is a bright illustration of the idea that in course of systems' synthesogenesis (and due to synthesogenesis) the variability of "elements" of the extending system grows at different levels of evolution. Thus it becomes obvious that studying manifestations of a person as an active "element" of developing systems (L.I. Antsyferova) must be based upon the principles describing the systems' aspects of human development in nature and society.

PRINCIPLE 2

Evolution of any developing system presumes the interplay of two contradictory tendencies - the tendency toward self-preservation and the tendency toward change of the given system. For instance, in biological systems *heredity* expresses the general tendency of the evolving system toward self-preservation, toward the transmission of undistorted genetic information from generation to generation, while *variability* manifests itself in the adjustment of different species to their environment. In social systems, the tendency toward self-preservation manifests itself in *social inheritance*, in the continuity of such typical forms of culture and social organization which provide adjustment of the given system to the situations already met during its evolution. Variability manifests itself in various non-standard, non-stereotyped adaptations of the system to unpredictable changes of situation, in the search of new information about the environment and in the construction of expedient behavior in it. *Individual variability of elements of a system is a condition for historical variation of the system as a whole.* The idea about individual variability of elements of a system as the basis for historical variation of populations, most explicitly articulated in biology by I.I. Shmalgauzen, reflects a universal regularity of development of any systems. The elements carrying individual variability may be:

an individual - in the system of the biological species;
a member of a tribe - in the system of the ethnic community;
a representative of a class - in the system of socioeconomic formation;
an adherent of a scientific school - in the system of the professional scientific community etc.

A person, being included in each of these systems, inherits system features typical for them and at the same time acts as a carrier of historical variability of these systems as a whole. Typical generic system qualities of a human being express the tendency of the evolving system toward self-preservation underlie various manifestations of human activity: stereotypes of behavior, reproductive thinking, habits, sets - labeled in psychology *adaptive* forms of activity. Variable and unique human qualities expressing the tendency toward change emerge in the course of synthesogenesis and manifest themselves in manifold forms of human activity such as creativity, imagination and self-realization, described as *productive* types of activity. The evolutionary meaning of adaptive types of activity is not only maintaining balance with the environment, homeostasis, survival. The main criterion of adaptation is providing the continuity of existence of an individual - his/her living in a succession of subsequent generations (I.I. Shmalgauzen), rather than just actual survival of an individual in a given environment.

PRINCIPLE 3

The principle of increasing influence of redundant system elements at the choice of the further direction of its development. A general characteristic of mechanisms of systems' development in the course of evolution has been proposed by N.N. Moiseyev. Besides *mechanisms of adjustment*, ensuring stability of the evolving system in specific environmental conditions, he distinguishes special *mechanisms of bifurcation*. The latter express the tendency of the evolving system toward change, and come into play in case of sharp changes in the environment, crises in the life of a system. One of the most important features of the systems' development under the control of mechanisms of adjustment is the *predictability* of the future behavior and development of these systems. Unlike mechanisms of adaptive development, a characteristic of bifurcation mechanisms is the *uncertainty* of the future of the system, i.e., unpredictability of the further development of the system which would follow after a crisis, or which new variant of evolution would be selected. Once the bifurcation mechanism starts to function, the behavior of the system cannot be deduced from its past (from heredity, genes, past experience etc.). Belgian chemist I. Prigogine, developing similar views on evolution of systems in nature and society, points out that *under conditions of instability, i.e., disequilibrium in the critical point of the system's life, its future cannot be predicted because any event or action that is negligible under regular conditions may entail changes of the whole system and the history will take another course.* Adaptive mechanisms functioning in social systems are connected with providing the person's stability, his/her typical predictable behavior in the group. Bifurcation mechanisms are inherent in the person's individual behavior in different problem or conflict situations. In the turning points of social life, individual deeds that may be negligible in other circumstances may cause a transformation of the society, become a spur to the coming of a new unpredictable phase in the development of culture.

Within the descriptions of human *system-functional* qualities, apparent in the stereotypical adaptive forms of behavior, these are characterized as sociotypical manifestations of personality in a social system. Characterizing *system-integrative* features of a person emerging in unpredictable situations, which cannot be managed on the basis of stereotypical behavior, the notion "personal *individuality*" is used. This distinction allows intertwined tendencies toward preservation and change, inherent in life activity of a person, considered as an "element" of various developing systems. Due to such a understanding of the terms "personality as a type" and "personality as an individuality" it also becomes possible to link sociotypical manifestations of a person to the realization of typical socially inherited programs of a given social community. At the same time, it allows singling out unique manifestations of personality which finally ensure the historical variability of this community. And most important is that this distinction helps to express the evolutionary meaning of personal individuality: manifestations of individuality mean potentialities of infinite lines of the creative evolutionary process of life. The analysis of the nature of individuality, and its functional significance in the evolutionary process results in the formulation of principles of the systems' historical-evolutionary approach to the human being which concerns the issues of self-development of various systems and of the relation between tribal adaptive strategy of development of these systems and non-adaptive strategy of development of their elements bearing individual variability.

PRINCIPLE 4

In any evolving system there are redundant nonadaptive elements, relatively independent of regulating influence of different forms of control, which ensure the system's self-development in case of unforeseen changes in the conditions of its existence. Various forms of activity of such "elements", included in evolving systems, do not directly lead to pragmatic adaptive effects that would serve the needs of the given systems and provide their preservation and stability.

A striking example of the manifestation of phylogenetic sprouts of nonadaptive activity in biological systems are animal games. Many biologists and ethnologists compete with each other, trying to better emphasize in the characteristics of animal games' uselessness for their biological adaptation. Playing behavior of animals is called "redundant", "illusory", "waste actions", "vacuum activity" etc. In fact, playing activity does not entail a direct adaptive effect. But by virtue of this feature, inherited forms of behavior are sharpened before they stand the trial of natural selection (K.E. Fabri). Thus the game creates the greatest possibilities for unlimited manifestation of an organism's individual variability and thereby for the accumulation of activity experience in case of a change of the conditions of existence of the given biological species.

The ideas of preadaptive nonutilitarian activity helps to highlight such a complicated question as the problem of change in the way of life, underlying the transition from the animal way of life to the qualitatively different one - that of Homo Sapiens. Based on careful analysis of anthropological and archaeological materials, well-known archaeologist G.P. Grigoriev comes to the conclusion that it is difficult to clearly distinguish between Homo Sapiens and other species of the genus Homo with the help of the so-called "tools criterion". It follows from these facts that at the same time as the Homo Sapiens there were other species which possessed vertical gait, big brain, advanced morphology of both extremities and, most importantly, provided themselves with food using tools made of stone, bone and wood. At the same time, among other hominid lines of evolution, as the joint research of archaeologists and psychologists show, only Homo Sapiens possessed such forms of preadaptive activity as deliberate burials, "bear caves", pictures and drawings which have been representing behavioral forms as though unnecessary for the species at the given moment, but defining its future evolution (A.G. Asmolov, S.A. Smirnov, M.V. Tendriakova). The question about the origins of Homo Sapiens in anthropogenesis is thus linked with the search of preadaptive redundant behavioral forms existing alongside with making and using tools.

Unique material for the understanding of evolutionary meaning of preadaptive activity in the history of different cultures can be found in M.M. Bakhtin's classical studies of carnival culture, in D.S. Likhachev's studies of the laughter culture in ancient Russia, and a series of Y.M. Lotman's works on the typology of culture. In these studies two features of preadaptive carnival or laughter social actions were outlined:

Laughter social actions, actions of fool or "yurodivy" ("God's fool") are allowed in the evolving system of the given culture and are relatively independent of social control that eliminates deviations from social standards inherent in the given culture;

In laughter social actions, socially inherited forms of relationships, typical for the given culture, are put into question; other variants of development of the culture are sought, other desirable reality is constructed.

Laughter social actions made it possible, in the frame of medieval culture to practice at the same time the behavior being qualified as sinful, illicit, and legal (Y.M. Lotman). The different nature and evolutionary meaning of adaptive and non-adaptive activities in the developing culture of the Middle Ages becomes evident in M.M. Bakhtin's comparison of an official feast and a carnival. Later, the ideas of M.M. Bakhtin were included by Y.M. Lotman into the context of his semiotic conception of culture. Lotman specially emphasized that *every culture as a self-developing system should be supplied with the "mechanisms to produce uncertainty"*. Due to uncertainty entering into a strictly determined cultural system, the given culture acquires a necessary *resource of internal variability,* becomes more sensitive, more ready for transformations in case of social crises (Y.M. Lotman). If we look through the prism of these ideas at the social carnival and laughter actions, at the acts of fools and "witches", the deeds of heretics, the phenomenon of odd "surplus people", it turns out that preadaptive acts of this kind, seemingly redundant from the viewpoint of the adaptive functioning of social community form a necessary condition for the historical changeability of this community and its evolution. Laughter social actions seem as if they care that this culture would not come to a dead end in its development, would not attain equilibrium, equal to immobility and death. They create an unstable absurd world of the "confused sign system" in which fantasies and cock-and-bull stories reign and the heroes do unexpected things.

Deeds of heretics, as well as social laughter actions of fools, bring uncertainty into a culture, deprive it of its stability and thus let out the tendency toward change in the social community. But unlike laughter social actions, these deeds fall under the eliminating influence of social control. The variants of evolution of culture proposed by them don't fit into the social system and therefore get stopped or rationalized by it. When the deeds of "surplus people" are being rationalized, they are often classified as social laughter actions, "artificial", foolish and therefore permitted.

The described spectrum of preadaptive activity manifestations of personality as the subject for activity is a necessary stage of the system's self-development and increases the possibilities of its evolution.

Thus, at different levels of functioning of the human being as an "element" of developing systems - both at the level of individual in a biological population and at the a level of personality as an individual member of a social community - preadaptive redundant forms of activity stand out which express the tendency toward change and thus appear as necessary points of the process of evolution of the given systems. In the turning points in the life of evolving systems (biological cataclysms, social crises) the significance of non-adaptive activity of the elements, included in these systems, increases and reveals its evolutionary meaning. Thus, for example, seemingly surplus non-adaptive actions of Giordano Bruno, who went to the bonfire for the sake of his beliefs, appear as the price for the adaptation of the evolving social community as a whole, for its progress. In that regard, a question about the fate of non-adaptive actions and their results in course of development of various systems is justified: can the actions, bearing the tendency of a system to change, to transform from non-adaptive into adaptive ones? What are the circumstances under which such changes of functional significance of an act in the systems' development may occur in evolution?

PRINCIPLE 5

A necessary condition for the development of different kinds of systems is the contradiction (conflict or harmonic interaction) between adaptive forms of activity, directed at the realization of the generic program, and the manifestations of activity of the elements bearing individual variability. From this principle of the systems' historical-evolutionary approach to human being as an active "element" of different systems, the following complementary statements follow:

The contradiction between the motives of individuality's activity appearing as a conflict or harmonic interaction with the ideals and norms of the social community can be resolved either through actions and activities transforming the generic program of the social community or through different transformations of motives of individuality in its interaction with the community. In case the contradiction has the character of harmonic interaction, actions and activities of the individuality entail further progress of the community. If the contradiction appears as a conflict, the activity of individuality may entail transformation of the generic program of the community and change the direction of the evolutionary process of the system.

Upholding one's motives and values by individuality proceeds as self-realization occurring in activity and leads either to the further development of the given culture or to generation of forms and products of another culture in the course of reality transformation.

Non-adaptive activity of an individuality degrades into adaptive activity with regard to the given community when norms and values created by this activity in the course of self-realization become norms and values of the corresponding culture. In this process the individuality's activity ceases to fulfil the function of change of the given system and begins to fulfil the function of its preservation and stabilization. For example, deeds of historical personalities proclaiming a new faith in the beginning are sometimes persecuted as they introduce disturbance, uncertainty into their contemporary culture. However, later, in case they succeed and their variant of evolution of the culture wins, these deeds become a standard and turn to stereotypes. As a result, they become carriers of system preservation function, beginning to eliminate or rationalize manifestations of activity of other individualities as carriers of other lines of evolutionary processes.

The idea of harmony of contrasts as the moving force of personality development was used by L.I. Antsyferova for the explanation of some forms of interaction (or cooperation) between different components of psychological organization of personality as an independent system, for example, harmonic contradiction between the desired and the achieved, etc. The systems historical-evolutionary approach to personal individuality analyses harmonic interaction, originating as a result of incongruity between "just known" ideals and group values, on the one hand, and ideals that became genuine motives for a group member. Individuality, being motivated by significant values, struggles for these values being not only formally recognized by the group, but really motivating the group's joint activity. Upholding these values, individuality as though pushes the group toward quicker progress on the accepted path of evolution, and sets a zone of proximal development. Sometimes people displaying activity that exceeds the utilitarian one are asked: "Well, do you need that most of all?". Thanks to the changes introduced into the generic program of a social community by non-utilitarian activity, this program of evolution comes true.

The actions of individuality often don't fit the canonical image of a "reasonable person", always acting rationally. In the history of culture, besides the image of "reasonable person" another standard of "individuality" emerged, its features being explicitly transmitted in myths and folklore of different peoples about their cultural heroes and their "twins", "dubbing fools" (E.M. Meletinsky). Mythological cheats (Y.I. Manin) and tricksters also belong to such "dubbing fools". V.N. Toporov analyzed an image of the trickster in Siberian folklore. On the basis of that material he discovered the role of individual behavior in the resolution of contradictions in the behavior of a social group.

The first individual feature characteristic of a trickster's behavior is setting up *supergoals*, i.e., goals transcending the regular circle of goals of a social group, which has elaborated standard typical actions for achieving them. The special character of goal setting by the individuality, shown in a folklore image of the trickster, leads to other features of his social portrait such as readiness to learn an unusual behavior; deviation from common norms and even their violation; unmotivated actions from the standpoint of common sense; the possibility of changing his outlook and moving freely through time and space; disinterestedness; searching for his unique chance on uncommon paths which are regarded by the collective consciousness as wrong and ineffective (V.N. Toporov). Quite an important feature of "mythological cheats" and cultural heroes, be they literary images like Don Quixote or Hodja Nasreddin wandering in the early Middle Ages vagrant poets, is their lack of rootedness in some social layer, their mobility in the culture. They do not simply move in geographical space, but travel in the social space of their time, destroying estate partitions, stable life order subordinated to rigid social control. These social nomads introduce uncertainty, revolt calmness, because they don't live a settled social life. They slip out from the influence of that or another centralized social control, dropping out of the rational picture of the world at large.

At the same time, the cultural heroes or tricksters oriented towards exclusive and unpredictable solutions help the social community to survive when it meets in its history situations requiring paradoxical decisions. The trickster of Russian folklore, Ivanushka the Fool, ceases to be a fool when a magical frog turns into Princess Maria. In such situations his tendency to paradoxical decisions comes forth, and he leaves the situation a brave (in public opinion) of "all honored people" as well. Sometimes individual behavior of fools or tricksters is described as opposition to normal behavior, as antinorm or anticulture. This destructive characteristic of the image of "fool" or "trickster" is incomplete. V.N. Toporov points out that the trickster in a critical situation finds *uncommon* ways out of it, *other* paths for the development of a social group, rather than automatically changing common norms in the culture of behavior to rejected ones. Ivanushka the Fool wins because he finds paradoxical ways to escape from hopeless situations, and thus becomes a public hero.

All these features are characteristic of the image of tricksters and cultural heroes in the myths and folklore of different cultures. In real life, there is a trickster or cultural hero, in every person that manifests itself in situations requiring to choose and set up supergoals, to resolve conflicts with the social group and oneself, to seek non-standard ways of development. Sometimes such a characteristic of individuality in the historical-evolutionary approach is perceived as an exocentric evaluation of the transpersonal or impersonal nature of the inner "Self", reducing genuine human essence to the role of trickster or fool (see A.B. Orlov: *Psychology of personality and human essence: Paradigms, projections, practice.* Moscow, 1995, p. 65). In this connection it is necessary to explain that we are talking about mastering of cultural standards, identification with which helps to master uncommon forms of behavior in critical situations. Therefore it is not the human essence that is reduced to the role of fool or cultural hero, but co-participation with the cultural hero or fool that allows the individuality to master a critical situation, to uphold the chosen meaningful image of the future and to provide the developing social system with other uncommon variants of its further development.

DISSEMINATING SELECTION AS A HYPOTHETICAL MECHANISM OF EVOLUTION IN ANTHROPOSOCIOGENESIS

Formulation of universal regularities of developing systems leads of necessity to a search for specific regularities of evolution in anthroposociogenesis. As an airplane taking-off into the sky does not violate the Laws of Gravity, according to L.M. Vekker's apt expression, the beginning of the social history of humankind does not cancel the laws of its natural history.

In discussions about the role of evolutionary regularities in the history of humankind, two contrasting points of view have arisen.

The first viewpoint, close to social-Darwinism, is based on the belief that natural selection still functions as the main moving force of evolution. Along with stupid ideological consequences, this position leads to absurd biological conclusions, for example, to a subordination of human morphophysiological development to the laws of natural selection in its biological variant and, from that, to the prediction of an appearance of the new human species in due course. Well-known biologists B.L. Astaurov, A.A. Bayev, D.K. Beliayev, N.P. Bochkov noticed that "social-eugenics" and "social-Darwinism" have damaged biology itself by pulling down the development of genetics by being identified with political doctrines which have used science to justify destructive social phenomena. Even now in some social sciences, including psychology, science is confused with ideology using scientific data.

The second viewpoint which emerged in the criticism of social-Darwinism has led to the conclusion that any impact of biological evolution after the beginning of the social development of humankind has in fact disappeared. Such an extreme position, presuming confusion of morphophysiological evolution with evolution of a way of life, against which A.N. Severtsov protested, should logically lead to the negation of laws of natural development in the natural-historical process. F. Engels in his work "Dialectics of nature" emphasized that the laws of nature are more and more turning into historical laws but are not canceled out by the laws of human history. It would be absurd, as was already mentioned, to say that by looking at a flying airplane the Law of Gravity is violated. But it is approximately this very idea which is propagated by a viewpoint which refuses to study the transformations of evolutionary laws in course of the transition of humankind to social-historical way of life. "Biologically-oriented-thinking" is replaced with "socially-oriented-thinking". But the extreme positions converge.

The issue of forms of evolution transformed by the transition of humankind to a social-historical way of life can now be resolved hypothetically. But without these hypotheses, the general psychology of personality, psychology of individual differences, psychophysiology of individual differences and psychogenetics would find themselves in a Procrustean bed of anthropocentric paradigm of conceiving the human being, which would deduce the differences between one person and another from their bodily constitutions, according to K. Marx, would try to differentiate humans from animals by the size of ear lobe.

In 1906, Halton, a disciple of Pearson, started a series of research trying to determine the correlation between anthropometric characteristics of a skull, body and... intelligence. R. Meily notes that the results of these investigations were absolutely negative, i.e., correlation between the size of skull and intelligence was not detected. First intelligence (Pearson) and then personality were sought inside the skull, i.e., the logic of analysis moved the way of seeking correlations between external physical characteristics and mental aspects of a person. This logic is based on the anthropocentric paradigm of conceiving human beings by studying a person outside the society and outside its development. In this connection, extremely significant for the progress of the psychology of personality is both the change of logic of its conceiving human beings and making sense of the data of differential psychology in the context of historical-evolutionary regularities. Besides general systems aspects of human development in evolving systems, of great interest for the psychology of personality, is the hypothesis of the so-called "disseminating selection", advanced by V.P. Alekseyev in the context of historical anthropology. This kind of selection carefully supports human variability and accentuations in the conditions of a social-historical way of life. The disseminating selection in human populations differs qualitatively from those forms of selection which act in the biological evolution of other species. "... However wide a species may be spread, its adaptive possibilities are limited, and species with wide areas, adapted to diverse biotypes, make a minority. The human species has mastered practically the whole planet and represents perhaps the most pan-oikumenic species on Earth. But it automatically entails a wide range of variability in contemporary humans. The wide range of variability, which is necessary for the prosperity and vital stability of humans, is the result of multidirectional selection. Yet this multidirectionality proceeds not successively, like in animals, but simultaneously, at the same of time. This selection does not stabilize the variability of the species as a whole but, on the contrary, picks up and fixes each special variation. Almost always there is some appropriate place for it in the diverse and constantly varying natural and social environment; in some conditions any variation may gain advantage over another one. Therefore, selection in humans, which in the past was no doubt a forming force, in contemporary society is weakened and functions now in its disseminating form, rather than in the stabilizing one, and this disseminating form of selection becomes more and more expressed. This form of selection offers no reasons to speak of the directed changes of human species as a whole" (V.P. Alekseyev. *Human Being: Evolution and taxonomy*. 1985, p. 110-111).

V.P. Alekseyev's hypothesis for the disseminating action of selection under the conditions of a human living in society, and of its support of variability explains a wide variance of different individual's properties and sets a search vector for the evolutionary meaning of different endowments, temperament, and constitutional features. The disseminating selection of a person's individual's properties in the conditions of a social way of life acts as a moment of social progress, a tendency toward increasing the variability of persons as potentialities for the creative process of cultural development.

* * *

The principles of the historical-evolutionary approach to the psychology of personality formulated above, make it possible to see the universal regularities of biogenesis, sociogenesis, ontogenesis and persogenesis. They also provide the criterion to evaluate which directions of the psychology of personality will develop within the psychological stepping over disciplinary boundaries. However, biogenetical, sociogenetical and persogenetical orientation in the psychology of personality would remain like parallel lines in Euclidean geometry rather than intersected lines in Lobachevsky's geometry without involving the principles of the activity theory approach. Therefore with regard to the principles of psychological analysis in the activity theory approach ([5]; [6]; [22]) and the scheme of systems determination of personality development ([2]; [5]; [6]; [23]; [25]), the perspectives of studying concrete mechanisms of transformation of individual properties and the social-historical way of life in a person's relations to the world, in the stream of activity, are outlined in this work.

CHAPTER 4

EVOLUTIONARY ASPECTS OF THE PROPERTIES OF HUMAN INDIVIDUAL AND THEIR ROLE IN THE REGULATION OF PERSON'S BEHAVIOR

Setting up a question about the evolutionary meaning of differences in the properties of the human individual in the developing systems in the context of historical-evolutionary approach leads to the distinction of two different directions in psychological research - the phenomenographical and the historical-evolutionary one.

PHENOMENOGRAPHICAL ORIENTATION IN PERSONALITY INVESTIGATIONS.

Phenomenographical orientation in personality investigations, embodying the paradigm of classical rational thinking, is inherent in different directions of the psychology of personality as, for example, constitutional psychology (E. Kretschmer, W. Sheldon, K. Konrad), differential psychology (R. Cattell, H. Eysenck, J. Guilford), characterology (F. Lersch), personology (H. Murray), humanistic psychology (A. Maslow).

Firstly, these different directions converge in their *formal* characteristic of individual differences as unique, original features of a "single" person, rather than a concentrated expression of integrated systems features of a person existing due to the way of life in the given culture and to previous history.

Secondly, these directions are explicitly or implicitly based on the two premises of studying personality structure in present-day psychology. The first one is an implicit identification of personality structure with the structure of a physical object, for example, with the anatomical structure of an organism. This way of thinking pushes researchers towards atomic analysis of personality, the analysis "by elements" (the second premise), which decomposes the subject of research into elements that lose the properties inherent in this subject as a whole (L.S. Vygotsky). Vivid examples of such an approach to personality structure are the theories where this structure is mechanically composed from a set of different factors, parameters of personality traits or blocks of temperament, motivation, past experience, character etc.

Thirdly, the phenomenographical tendency in studying personality limits oneself to listing various traits, constitutions, types of temperament, types of higher nervous activity, tendencies, emotional experiences, abilities and motives which distinguish one person from another. Such representatives of the various directions in differential psychology as R. Cattell, H. Eysenck and J. Guilford play a game "Who has less?" making the lists of "descriptive variables", "factors", "parameters" of personality where with equal rights cyclothymia, bohemianism, practicism, conformity, emotionality, sociability, etc. (up to 171 "descriptive variables" - R.Cattell) are introduced. An object paradigm is easily visible behind such studies of individual differences borrowed from natural sciences, that describes a human being in his/her psychological characteristics in the same way as in his/her physical characteristics. This object paradigm, transforming the human being into an isolated single "object with various properties", is largely transformed when psychologists proceed to the subject paradigm of individual differences analysis and build methodical procedures taking into account a person's activity and human activity nature (A.G. Shmelev). Yet the common denominator for both "objective" and "subjective" paradigms is that in their framework the question is never put, what has brought to existence the surprising variability of personality, the variety of its traits? In other words, within the context of a phenomenographical study of individual differences the researchers limit themselves by setting up a question "how does the phenomenon occur?"; and much less often "why does it occur?". The main task of differential psychology solving the first question becomes the laborious description and "collecting" (A.V. Petrovsky) of a person's individual differences. Resolving the second question, researchers focus their attention on the mechanisms of personality functioning and, proceeding from early variants of the two-factor determination scheme, select the strategy of the analysis of personality structure. It is shown in the historical-evolutionary approach that by the object of study, by methodical procedures, terminology and, most important, by the choice of this or that variant of two-factor scheme of determination the following strategies of studying personality structure and the place of properties of the human individual in this structure are distinguished: constitutional-anthropometric strategy, "factor" strategy of studying personality traits, "block" strategy of studying personality structure; motivational-dynamic strategy of studying personality organization; behavioral-interactive strategy of studying personality organization (see [5]).

In these five outlined strategies of studying psychological organization of personality, despite all the differences in underlying theoretical positions, in the choice of "elements" of personality organization, methods assessment of traits, motives, temperament, i.e., different substructures of personality, a general tendency is manifested to locate "individual's" properties of a human being person in the basis of personality organization, to characterize them as its the basis or basal level. For example, in the humanistic psychology of A. Maslow (motivational-dynamic strategy) physiological needs (thirst, hunger) make the lowest level in the hierarchy of needs, and in such a contrast approach to the former as the conception of personality traits of J. Guilford ("factor" strategy) organic needs such as hunger, sexual urge etc. again belong to the "motivational factor A".

Actually, the hierarchical model of personality organization, despite the fact that its lowest level, i.e., an individual's properties of a person, is treated as the basis, the foundation upon which personality is built, has occasionally become in contemporary psychology one of the methodological premises for the sharp break between the general psychology of personality and differential psychophysiology (B.I. Kochubey). The location of the individual's properties of a person at the "ground floor" of personality structural organization and their studying outside evolutionary-historical process of development of the system, in which the person lives, entails either the absolutization of "primary" basal properties in the organization and dynamics of personality development or ignoring them while studying "upper" social levels of personality organization. It was the transformation of "individual's properties of a person" into the base, that led in fact to their shift into the periphery of the psychology of personality, as well as to the oppositions: "formal individual's characteristics - meaningful social characteristics of personality"; "energetic individual characteristics - informative social characteristics", that legalized the break between general psychology of personality and differential psychophysiology and the dualism of "biological" and "social" under the roof of the multistory organization of personality.

If we treat the individual properties of a person as functional-structural features, reflecting the history of the human species and being the premises for personality development in the social-historical way of living, they lose the illusory privilege of being the "original basis" of personality. Instead, the individual's properties become those real premises that, being transformed in course of joint activity, contribute to personality development in the system of social relations and into the evolutionary-historical process at large. They are not located "under", nor "above" social properties of personality, but in the concrete activity they may appear as both necessary premises of this activity, being improved in it; and as psychophysiological executive mechanisms of activity ensuring the achievement of its various goals, and as "means" that personality considers and masters in order to evaluate his/her capacities in the course of choosing tasks of different complexity. The introduction of joint activity as the basis of personality development to psychology does not make functional-structural features of an individual impersonal, on the contrary, it opens the way to the study of essential regularities of development and regulation of functional-structural properties of an individual in the evolving system of the social-historical way of life.

HISTORICAL-EVOLUTIONARY ORIENTATION IN THE STUDY OF HUMAN ORGANISMIC PROPERTIES AND THEIR ROLE IN THE REGULATION OF A PERSON'S BEHAVIOR

The question about the evolutionary meaning of individual differences between people, the question "what for" (N.A. Bernstein) do they arise in an evolving system, has only recently have begun to be raised in this or that variant in the analysis of person's organismic properties (B.G. Ananiev, A.I.

Belkin, N.N. Bragina, T.A. Dobrokhotova, V.A. Geodakian, T.V. Karsaevskaya, I.S. Kon, P.V. Simonov, V.V. Frolkis). In this research the tendency to analyze human individual's properties in the framework of historical-evolutionary process comes out. The analysis of the facts obtained in this research on the basis of the principles of an activity theory approach in the psychology of personality makes it possible to depict the mechanisms of transformation of a human individual's properties in the course of a person's building his/her way of life.

To characterize the specificity of problem setting within the framework of historical-evolutionary orientation and the choice of concrete research strategy, examples from the psychology of sexual differences and from the analysis of the place of organic urges in human behavior regulation can be mentioned.

In the field of the *psychology of sexual differences*, the role of biological sex in personality development, the break between biogenetic research (J. Money, J. Hutchinson), sociogenetic research (M. Mead) and cognitive-personological research (R. Sears, L. Kohlberg) remains stable. In the context of the historical-evolutionary approach, the problems of the psychology of sexual differences are originally set in a different way. This is the problem of social differentiation of roles, connected with the evolution of society and, first of all, with the sociocultural evolution of the institution of family; the problem of influence of joint activity and way of life on the genesis of sexual differences in the development of a child's personality, formation of his/her psychological sex, and the development of educational strategies with allowance for the psychology of sexual differences; the problem of the reasons for the emergence of sexual dimorphism and its adaptive function in the historical-evolutionary process; the problem of distortions in the formation of a person's psychological sex and the development of methods of active social-psychological rehabilitation of behavior deviations connected with sexual dimorphism. It would be more exact to speak of logic of problem setting as of tendency, rather than as a firmly established research direction in the psychology of sexual differences.

For example, it was shown in this research that sexual dimorphism does not determine unambiguously the person's psychological sex, nor is it a universal property of any biological species from the very beginning. Sexual dimorphism has a phylogenetic history and evolutionary meaning. The idea of the evolutionary meaning of sexual dimorphism can cast light on some problems of the psychology of sexual differences. In the context of the *synthetic theory of evolution* by I.I. Shmalgauszen, the hypothesis is developed by V.A. Geodakian that there are operative and conservative subsystems in any evolving system providing both stability and evolution of any developing systems. The operative subsystem provides variability of the system in its relations with the environment. It adjusts more flexibly to changes, but is also more fragile and subject to destruction. The conservative subsystem is to save and transmit parental properties to posterity unchanged. It is more stable and better adapted for the solution of standard tasks. Female individuals in the system of different biological species provide invariance, stability of the "inertial" genetic kernel of population in the course of selection; male individuals, being the "operative subsystem", embody the tendency to variability. Different variants of development are tested upon the male individuals. If these variants turn out to be successful they are first consolidated in the course of selection by the male individuals and then transmitted to the female individuals, as though getting into the long-term "genetic memory" of the species. The ideas by V.A. Geodakian explain, for example, the facts of higher mortality of males as compared to females in the process of evolution, etc. These ideas are important, first of all, because they pose the question of why does sexual dimorphism appear in the process of evolution (V.A. Geodakian. *System-Evolutionary Treatment of Brain Asymmetry. In: Systems research*, 1986).

The logic of the historically-evolutionary approach comes out very boldly when studying *the role of various kinds of organic urges in the regulation of a person's behavior*. Three different attempts to take into account organic urges, including both "deficiency needs" and "growth needs", belong to P.V. Simonov, S.A. Arutyunov and V.A. Ivannikov. P.V. Simonov attempts to consider the problem of urges in the context of the evolutionary approach, reminding us that the elementary unit of evolution is a population rather than a separate individual. He, following A.A. Ukhtomsky, also notes that with the emergence of a social way of life "...the main tendency in the development of motives(needs - A.A.) is an expansion towards mastering the environment by extending the space-time scale (chronotop), rather than reduction as the tendency toward "defense" from the environment, reaching balance with it, and relief from inner tension. This tendency of *development* ("growth needs", using the terms of Western authors) can be realized only due to its dialectic unity with the capacity of living systems towards *preservation* of themselves and the results of their activity results, due to the satisfaction of "deficiency needs" (Simonov P.V., Ershov P.M. *Temperament. Character. Personality.* M., 1984. p. 93-94). Thus P.V. Simonov divides the motivational sphere of personality into two sectors, one of which provides homeostasis and expresses in the evolutionary aspect the general tendency toward the preservation of the species, while another one, including, for example, cognition and the needs of cognition, expresses the tendency of the development of the species at the level of a separate individual. An analysis of the problem of individual urges from the viewpoint of an evolutionary approach is an important step in the study of the nature of needs.

At the same time, such an analysis remains in a sense within the framework of the division of individual needs into biological needs subordinated to the regularities of natural selection and social needs inherent in a human being. A somewhat different version for analysis of biological needs was proposed by the well-known ethnographer S.A. Arutyunov. He notes that already at the level of purely biological phenomena, for example, childbirth, sexual acts etc., some ethnic distinctions stipulated by the way of life appear. These ethnic distinctions concern the methods and ways by means of which natural needs are satisfied, i.e., the external side of behavior, while the actions themselves remain constant, universal and invariant. A person can sleep on a floor or in a shelter, to keep awake, but there is no alternate acting in the sphere of natural behavior (not to sleep at all). In the opinion of S.A. Arutiunov, "natural" models of behavior differ from sociocultural behavior in that they do not have alternatives (to eat or not to eat, to sleep or not to sleep, etc.). Execution of "natural" behavior driven by common human individual's needs assumes no choice of the final goal of behavior and social way of life concerns just the way of attaining the goal.

The third point of view is that organic urges of an individual do not characterize the individual as it is, but rather express the relations, systems structural-functional qualities of the individual in a society (V.A. Ivannikov). Consistent elaboration of this point of view leads to the conclusion that a social-historical way of life of a person in society transforms both individual urges and the means of their satisfaction. The sphere of human needs cannot be divided into "deficiency needs" and "growth needs", and the tendencies toward preservation and change of a developing system relate to any manifestations of human motivation. Whether the mechanism of "tension reduction" acts or not, depends on the place of concrete urges in the structure of human activity, rather than on their "natural" or "social" origins.

So, in a standard situation, this or that incentive, say, water, occupies the structural place of a collateral condition for the realization of activity, actualizes an impulsive operational set subordinated to the mechanism of "tension reduction". In another situation (say a traveler lost in a desert), the same incentive, water, may rise up to the level of a motive that actualizes a sense set ([1]). In the course of societal development, a number of values inevitably reach the status of object-incentives and operational impulsive sets of personality appear to be enough for their achievement. For example, clinical observations of patients with anorexia nervosa, whose motive of voluntary starvation becomes the sense-making motive of their personality (M.A. Kareva), as well as experimental investigations in the situation of medically prescribed starvation showed that the moving force of food urge on the person's behavior depends on the level of sets (sense-related, goal, operational impulsive) in which these urges manifest themselves (A.G. Asmolov, M.A. Kareva, S.I. Kuriachy).

The regularities, illustrated above using the material of food urges, have a more general nature and relate to all the organic needs of an individual. These urges, as they are, can be referred neither to "deficiency needs" nor to "growth needs". Whether the dynamics of organic urges would follow the homeostatic principle of "tension reduction" or there would be a tendency toward change behind the manifestations of organic urges - depends on the *place occupied by these urges both in the structure of separate activity of the person and in the hierarchy of motives of the personality as a whole*. In the case where organic urges come out at the level of conditions of action, i.e., in the stereotyped forms of activity, they express the general tendency toward preservation and are subordinated to the mechanisms of homeostasis and tension reduction. However, under certain circumstances, organic urges can take the place of sense-making motives of a person's activity, which embody the tendency of a system toward change in this or that critical situation, for example, in the situation of a deliberately chosen hunger-strike. In this case organic urges are included within the context of non-adaptive behavior of individuality, upholding this or that life goals and ideals. Thus individuality can consciously consider an alternative "to eat or not to eat", "to drink or not to drink", "to be or not to be", concerning ultimate vital goals of behavior. The social-historical way for the life of personality in society rebuilds the regularities for functioning of organic urges of the individual, the dynamics of which depends on their place in the structure of a person's activity and which, being transformed in the activity, become the result of a person's behavior rather than just its premise.

Based on an analysis of the manifestations of various individual properties in a person's life, we can list five general features of behavior regulation.

First. With all the variety and specificity of individual's properties, as well as their variability (whether it be age sensitivity, emotional excitability, introversion, neuroticism) the individual's properties characterize mainly formal-dynamic features of a person's behavior, the energetic aspect of mental processes (I.M. Paley, V.K. Gerbachevsky). So, for example, as V.S. Merlin notes, temperament does not determine the contents of a personality's relation to reality, but influences only the form of this relation. One should never forget this. Otherwise there is a danger of keeping to the beaten track of construction of substantial typologies of personality on the basis of formal properties of the individual. Such typologies proceed from the methodological premise that ascribes the property "to be a person" to the individual's nature itself. At first sight this substitution is hard to notice, because in the everyday understanding "individual" is identified with "person". From such a coincidence follows the substitution of the individual for the person, the appearance of individual-natural fetishism. Then on the basis of individual's properties personality typologies are construed. It is even not so important what would be taken as the basis for the classification: constitution (E. Krechmer), somatotype (W. Sheldon) etc.

However, these or those individual properties, being transformed in the course of activity, can change their formal-dynamic features. Thus a need as an organic premise of the person's activity, relates to an individual's properties manifested in activation and arousal, poorly selective searching activity, i.e., in the formal-dynamic characteristics of a person's activity. When an organic urge meets an object, the need is transformed into a motive for the person's activity and begins to determine the direction of behavior. The formal-dynamic characteristic of an urge thus does not disappear but begins to come out in another form - in the form of a moving force of a person's motive.

Second. The individual's properties (type of nervous system, constitution, endowments, extraversion or intraversion etc.) determine a range of possibilities to choose this or that activity within the limits having no essential social adaptive significance. The extraversion then just increases the probability of choosing this or that social role connected with the process of communication (speaker, actor, teacher etc.), actually made by companions in his joint activity, rather than by the individual him/herself. Speech defects, on the contrary, can lessen the probability of choosing this kind of social role. Whether or not an appropriate social role would be chosen or not, depends, however, not on the speech defect or extraversion itself, but rather on the attitude of both joint activity companions and the person him/herself to these properties, be they original or emerged as a result of an organic disease.

Third. Literally, when the person is told by other people about his/her individual's properties, these properties become signified, turn into "signs". The transformation of an individual's properties into "signs" changes their function in the regulation of behavioral dynamics and personality development. As a result of this transition, the person gains an image of his/her individual properties and the possibility of deliberate control over his/her body in the same way as over the objects of outer reality. In particular, the "internal picture of disease" (R.A. Luria), the image of one's own disease, often developed in the course of a dialogue with a physician, - this is a typical example of "signification" of this or that pathological malfunctioning of an individual's properties which only by virtue of becoming "signs", begin to participate in the control over a person's behavior. *The principles of mediation and signification* (L.S. Vygotsky, A.R. Luria) relate not only to higher forms of behavior. *If individual properties become "signs", they become subordinate to conscious self-regulation and, thereby, can potentially be not only premises, but also the result of personality development.* The person, through transformation of the outer world, can gain the power not only over outer reality, but also over the manifestations of one's own individual's properties. An individual nature in this sense is created as the world is transformed by a person. So, the peculiarities of constitution themselves do not determine personality development. However, they can become "signs" which, being involved in the person's life, at times become almost the decisive factors in shaping the character of individuality. Being included into the dynamics of social relations, these "signs" turn into the "means" used by the person for the justification of a certain life position and his/her actions, for example, one's privilege of being an "exception" (S. Freud).

In borderline psychiatry the manifestations of a morbid belief in an imaginary physical defect are described, most frequently met in adolescence and juvenile age (M.V. Korkina). This disease has the name "dismorphophobia". "Signification" of imaginary defects by the patients can at first entail the impoverishment of interpersonal relations and then depersonalization, i.e., sharp disorders of self-consciousness, disintegration of self-image and loss of orientation in the environment. In the case of dismorphophobia, not only character, but also self-consciousness of the person suffers. However, the determination of personality disorders in dismorphophobia is in no way the determination by the two factors of "environment" and "heredity". It is not accidentally that dismorphophobia arises most often in youth, the age of the search for oneself. In this period a bad joke told by surrounding people can cause a fixation on the "imaginary defect", transform it into a "sign" that may begin to determine the choice of behavior by a girl or a boy, lead to impoverishment of relationships and then to self-consciousness disorders and the loss of one's Self. The dismorphophobia syndrome is significant because it demonstrates the influence of imaginary physical defects on the shaping of the character of the person through their becoming "signs" in the system of social relations, rather than direct determination of personality traits by the physical features of his/her constitution.

In some cases, constitutional defects become the "means" of justifying the exclusive role of a person in the society, in other cases they, through an evaluation by surrounding people, make the person fall out of the system of interpersonal relationships and cause self-consciousness disorders even in the absence of real defects (dismorphophobia); but sometimes, even heavy corporal defects, diseases confining the person to bed, are overcome by the person who succeeded in asserting the power of individuality over the properties of the individual. The features of constitution do not themselves predetermine the character of the person. They are "impersonal" premises of personality development, that can become "signs", "means" during the life span, and only being signified, they can entail the shaping of this or that manifestations of the person's individuality.

Fourth. In real life situations, many individual properties of the person appear as autonomously regulated subsystems of the individual subordinated to decentralized control. For example, thermal regulation of the organism, neurodynamic processes etc. in the course of evolution went the way of specialization, segregatiogenesis. This made it possible to release the central levels of regulation for solving the tasks faced in unforeseen situations. The ideas developed by M.M. Bongard demonstrate the limitations of the image of hierarchical centralized types of control in any self-regulating system, including the conceptions of personality organization that depict the individual's properties as the basis that regulates (E. Kretschmer, W. Sheldon) or is regulated by the superordinate social levels (for example, the level of "superego", according to S. Freud). Entering different social systems, the person is not necessarily granted with social or individual's systems qualities that are controlled from the single command post of "Ego", from one "center", watching over the subordination of these qualities, their reporting to higher command about the executed work. The person's behavior in different systems assumes the existence of polyphonic integrated centralized and decentralized behavior regulation (M.M. Bongard, D.A. Pospelov), allowing the autonomy and specialization of different subsystems involved in personality development. The advantage from the evolutionary viewpoint is provided by the combination of centralized and decentralized control of individual and social system features of the person. "... The decentralization, allowing the systems to work autonomously, has however one rather substantial defect... This defect is connected in that decentralized regulation requires increased time for adaptation. What can be done very quickly in the system upon receiving a uniform order from the center, if the central link receives information about environmental changes beforehand, would go very slowly in a decentralized system ... Therefore... there are as though two levels of control: decentralized and centralized. However, these levels do not duplicate one another. While the environment is nearly constant and suits the person, decentralized regulation is operating totally. Its separate subsystems function almost autonomously and do not interact much with each other. But suddenly a sharp change in the environment happens, threatening the person with unfavorable consequences. It is necessary to bring all the systems into a state of fighting readiness as soon as possible. How the centralized control acts rapidly, transferring the organism into a state of stress. The main feature of this response is its unspecificity. It acts in any dangerous situation and is directed at the interaction with all the subsystems of the organism. Thus, there is a rather interesting distribution of functions between the decentralized and the centralized parts of the system. In slowly changing or constant environments the decentralized part of control successfully copes with the adjustment to the attainment of the organism's global aims, while in the case of sharp changes of the environment an organism turns on some overall system" (Varshavsky V.I., Pospelov D.A. *An orchestra plays without the conductor*: Reflections on the evolution of some technical systems and their control. Moscow, 1984. p. 174-175).

The ideas of the combination of the centralized and the decentralized control have direct relations to the problems of relationships between different social properties of personality in different social communities and the relationships between individual and social qualities of a person. In fact, the individual properties come out most often just as the premises of personality development because they are adjusted to a relatively stable ecological system. Thereby under the conditions of a social-historical way of life they, in a sense, stay in a constant ecological situation. As a result, they have acquired large specialization in the course of evolution and have won the right for autonomous functioning within the personality system. "Centers", that control sociotypical behavior, are less autonomous. But here also the prevailing way of behavior control is neither centralization nor decentralization, but rather the combination of decentralized control, serving stereotyped sociotypical behavior, and centralized control of the individual behavior. In the case of a sharp change of the ecological situation, the mode of autonomous control of individual's properties can be replaced by the mode of centralized control. Unlike all other biological species, every human is potentially able to find, to invent "sign-means" that he or she may use to take relatively autonomous subsystems of individual properties under deliberate conscious control. Still in a greater degree this rule relates to the stereotyped sociotypical behavior that serves the individuality of the person in typical situations and because of its superspecialization fails in those unforeseen situations when it is necessary to make a decision, a personal choice.

The rule of a combination of centralized and decentralized control of personality subsystems, that is, of the existence of non-specialized general subsystems and specialized autonomous subsystems of the individual, has fundamental significance for a search for those general psychophysiological mechanisms of temperament that participate in supplying substantial aspects of a person's behavior. The more autonomous is a subsystem of individual properties, the more likely it is subordinated to the decentralized control mode and, accordingly, the less its part in maintenance of regulation of a person's behavior comes out. It follows that the direction for a search of various general psychophysiological functional systems, underlying behavior in unforeseen non-specific situations (research of B.M. Teplov and V.D. Nebylitsyn), is more perspective than the search for links of a person's behavior with more autonomous phylogenetically ancient subsystems of decentralized regulation of the human organism (E. Kretschmer, W. Sheldon).

At present, in the psychophysiology of individual differences the following problems of the study of temperament appear. The first relates to the analysis of organic (neurophysiological, biochemical) mechanisms carrying psychodynamic peculiarities of temperament in a person's behavior. The main direction in the elaboration of this problem goes from types of higher nervous activity to an analysis of integral manifestations of brain activity, to studying general properties of the nervous system (B.M. Teplov, V.D. Nebylitsyn and others). The second problem relates to the study of adaptive capacities of temperament in the process of evolution.

Studying the role of temperament in the process of Homo Sapiens evolution or, as they say sometimes, the issue of the place of temperament in adaptation of the individual, should not be confused with the "evaluative-ethical" approach to the analysis of temperament that has been criticized by B.M. Teplov. An "evaluative approach" to temperament contradicts the ideas of "disseminating selection", functioning in the historical-evolutionary process and supporting, saving quite different variations, that may have evolutionary meaning in this or that specific situations. Some manifestations of temperament tend to support the general tendency toward the preservation of an evolving system, its stabilization; others - the tendency toward change of this system providing large adaptive variability in extreme and critical situations.

Fifth. The use of individual's properties as "signs", "means", with the help of which the person masters and improves individual features, underlies the origins of "individual styles" in the ontogenesis of a person's behavior and opens large possibilities of compensation, correction of natural forms of an individual responding in learning various professions. This problem is connected with the issue of personality mastering one's individual's properties, including the features of temperament, as a special "means" for activity regulation. It leads to research on compensation mechanisms and individual style of activity as dependent on characteristics of temperament. In this framework temperament is being studied in the context of its use by the person as the subject of various kinds of activity, rather than as it is.

The psychological nature of regularities of the subject's mastering the properties of temperament, and also the fact that individual properties do not directly determine development of the person, but do it through their influence at methods of activity, its operational mechanisms, are investigated in the research of V.S. Merlin and E.A. Klimov. To understand the regularities of the use of the properties of temperament as the "means" of activity and compensatory possibilities of the person, the idea about *a zone of uncertainty* introduced by V.S. Merlin has fundamental significance. When choosing means and methods of attaining the goal of action, the subject usually has a field of variants of choice, rather than rigid tying to any single method of achieving the desired goal.

Research reveals the perspective for the study of psychodynamic properties of a person in the context of their use by the person as the subject of activity the dependence of mental stress on its place in the structure of activity (O.V. Ovchinnikova, N.I. Naenko), and investigations in sports psychology, studying anxiety, stress in extreme situations. In this sphere of applied research there is a shift to active methods of mastering individual properties such as "biological" feedback, autotraining, etc. With their help the person can "signify" his/her physiological states and by that learn to use them as psychological "means" of behavior self-regulation.

* * *

The general peculiarities of transformation of an individual's properties in ontogenesis of a human person point at the limitations of biogenetic orientation, reducing the process of development of the individual to the realization of a biologically preset program. In the conditions of a social-historical way of life, individual properties of a person appear not only as "impersonal" premises defining the formal-dynamic features of behavior and the range of possibilities to choose this or that activity within the limits of socially important adaptive significance. They are transformed during a person's life and, becoming "signs", can be used as "means" of mastering the person's behavior. Using these means, a person receives the possibility of compensating for this or that natural limitation and elaborates individual styles of activity. The contribution of individual properties to the maintenance of behavior regulation depends on the type of control - centralized or decentralized - to which individual subsystems, realizing various ways of human activity, are subordinated and on their place in the structure of the goal-directed activity of the person. At the same time, the individual's properties do not themselves influence personality development, but are mediated by the subject's way of acting, i.e., by the operational structure of his/her activity.

In general, the way of life of humankind leads to reorganization of regularities of the historical-evolutionary process, but just to reorganization, rather than to its full cancellation. Evolutionary regularities do not simply die out, but get radically transformed, the logic of reasons and moving forces of the evolutionary process also change radically. The individual properties of the person express, first of all, the tendency of a person, as an "element" in the developing system of society, toward preservation, providing wide adaptation of human populations in the biosphere. They can be explained mainly in the context of homeostatic models of adaptation especially when the most phylogenetically ancient levels of organization of the individual are concerned. However, the biology of the individual's development, his/her ontogenesis, in spite of an abundance of empirical facts, in the opinion of the famous biologist B.L. Astaurov, is still lacking. Its main difficulties are just that the individual's development proceeds within the context of a social way of life, that is not simply imposed on natural "substance" of a person but leads to the transformation of this natural "substance" in anthropogenesis, sociogenesis and in ontogenesis itself. In this regard, the regularities of biological evolution developed on the basis of phylogenesis in biology cannot be transferred onto the individual development of a person in ontogenesis. The question of the nature and the character of these regularities, including the influence of a social way of life and the person's life circle on ontogenetic development of the individual, still awaits solution.

CHAPTER 5

FROM THE SOCIOGENESIS TO THE PERSOGENESIS OF PERSONALITY

The subject of research in the historical-evolutionary approach in psychology is the history of evolution of a changing personality in the changing world. Therefore in this book the legitimacy of the view of the social world as the changing one is upheld in three complementary aspects: *historical time, social space and life circle of a person within the space of a given culture.* The first of these aspects could be labeled as the diachronic aspect, the second aspect - as the synchronic one, and the third - as the one integrating the first two aspects in studying personality development within a given culture. If in the analysis of regularities of personality development any of the indicated aspects is missed, then the "social environment" will turn from the source of personality evolution into an external social decor, an eternal and abstract "social factor" outside historical time and social space.

It is the sociogenesis rather than the "social environment" and even than "social situation of development" (L.S. Vygotsky) that is taken as initial coordinate system to solve the tasks of studying personality in the sociohistorical dynamics using the historical-evolutionary approach. What is meant by sociogenesis in psychology is the origin and evolution of personality and interpersonal relations, conditioned by the peculiarities of socialization in different historical epochs and different cultures [54].

In the case when psychology of personality investigates the role of personality in different historical epochs, i.e., the diachronic aspect of sociogenesis, it can compare the "pictures of the world" (A.Y. Gourevich) of people from different epochs with the particular "picture of the world" emerged in the life span of personality in the given epoch. If research on the psychology of personality is focused on the synchronic aspect of sociogenesis, then rituals, conventions, national character come to the front which reveals the specificity of the given culture in comparison with other contemporary cultures. The synchronical aspect of sociogenesis is of the greatest interest for the representatives of ethnic and cross-cultural psychology.

The historical-evolutionary approach attempts to outline a panorama of hitherto isolated research, illuminating mutual transitions between sociogenesis and persogenesis of personality, to allocate particular problems and to single out perspective directions for analysis of the developing personality in a changing world. While studying the processes of transition from sociogenesis to persogenesis the following tendency becomes obvious: while in the studies of sociologists, historians, culturologists and ethnographers attention is increasingly given to studying a person's mentality in different historical epochs and cultures (S.S. Averintsev, S.A. Aroutiunov, L.M. Batkin, Y.B. Bromley, A.Y. Gourevich, G.G. Diligensky, I.S. Kon, D.S. Likhachov, Yu.M. Lotman, E.S. Markarian and others), in psychology some works about sociogenesis of a person's behavior in the thirties (L.S. Vygotsky, A.N. Leontiev, A.R. Luria, D.B. Elkonin), were followed by many years of silence. In psychology, the symptoms of insufficient elaboration of the ideas of personality in the sociohistorical dynamics of different evolving systems are the torments of a delayed birth of various interdisciplinary borderline branches of science - ethnopsychology, historical psychology, palaeopsychology, as well as a predominance of laboratory procedures and tests lacking ecological validity over research on personality in a concrete historical social situation of development. It was only at the beginning of the seventies that papers making interdisciplinary bridges between the psychology of personality and other branches of human science started to appear. Due to a broad cycle of research in the rather young Russian social psychology, and new interdisciplinary research appearing on the borders with history, ethnography, semiology etc., general statements about the social determination of personality development are replaced by concrete conceptions of the human world. This means that which is acquired by a person and makes the contents of the social system qualities in the given culture, that which a personality acquires within the system of social relations. A key to the understanding of the mechanism of personality movement in the social system is the category of "social-historical way of life" being fruitfully elaborated in social sciences. The category "social-historical way of life", as well as the related ideas of the "social situation of development", first, enables removing the opposition "personality vs. society" and considering regularities for movement of "personality in the society"; second, makes it possible to analyze personality development as if at the crossing of three coordinates - the coordinates of historical time, social space and the life span of a personality in society.

The nature of time and its role in the determination of personality development are very poorly known in psychology. Classical research of qualitatively different structures of time in physical, geological, biospherical and social systems by V.I. Vernadsky have hardly touched psychology. In the same way psychology for a long time studied personality in "artificial worlds", "environments", being satisfied with the understanding of time, borrowed from classical mechanics. Any transformations of time in the history of culture or in the human mind, its thickening or acceleration have been interpreted as illusion, some "illusory" deviations from the physical time. In the activity theory approach, the thesis about the dependence of time on the systems within which the time is treated - inorganic nature, evolution of organic nature, sociogenesis of society, history of the person's life span, - has been formulated by S.L. Rubinstein. The elaboration of these ideas in the psychology of personality has only just recently begun (K.A. Abulkhanova, E.I. Golovakha, A.A. Kronik). In the research of E.I. Golovakha and A.A. Kronik the characteristics of various forms of determination of a person's life by time are given: "physical" or "chronological" time, to which the idea of time in the positivistically oriented cognitive psychology is still reduced; "biological" time, depending on the vital activity of biological systems, and studied first of all in works on biological life rhythms, biological clock; "historical" time conditioned by peculiarities of sociogenesis of concrete-historical communities (for example, who would today call a trip from Moscow to St.-Petersburg "travel", as A.N. Radischev did nearly two centuries ago?); "psychological" time of personality, being simultaneously a condition and a product of activity in a person's life span.

The axe of historical time of a person's way of life in the given society enables singling out the objective social regime, which is preset to a person - historically conditioned durability of childhood in the culture; the objective regime of change of play for study, study for work, characteristic of this typical way of life. Without taking historical time into account, one or another features of human activity, involving a child in a play or a study would seem "leading", stemming either from the child him/herself, or from the immediate social environment, which can hardly slow down or accelerate the historical pace of the way of life, but not change it within the frame of the given epoch. A question is raised, whether the duration of childhood is one of the criteria of the "height" of a civilization (A.V. Zaporozhets).

Along with the transition of a person's activity from the regime of consumption, appropriation of culture, to the regime of creativity, biological and historical time is more and more transformed to the psychological lifetime of personality that creates plans of his/her own and embodies his/her life program in the social way of life of the given society. In terms of L. Seve, the "lifetime" of the person is transformed into his/her "time for living".

Another coordinate of the way of life is social space, object reality, within which in a given interval of historical time various "institutes of socialization" (family, school, working collectives), large and small social groups exist, participating in the process of involving the personality into the social-historical experience through joint activity. In the fairy tale of Morice Metterlink "The Blue Bird" the kind elfin presents a magical diamond to children. One need only turn this diamond to become able to see the invisible souls of things. Subjects of human culture surrounding people do really have, as K. Marx put it, "social soul". And this "soul" is nothing but the field of meanings, existing in form of action schemes embodied in tools, in the form of roles, concepts, rituals, ceremonies, various social symbols and norms. A person becomes a personality only if he/she becomes involved through social groups into the stream of activity (rather than stream of consciousness!) and acquires in this way meanings externalized in the human world. That diamond is joint activity; a child turns it together with other people, usually being unaware of what he or she is doing, and sees "social souls" of things, acquiring his/her own "soul". In other words, in the surrounding world there is objectively a special social dimension, created by the cumulated human activity, - field of meanings. This field of meanings is what a separate individual finds as something "out-there-existing", perceived, acquired, as something included into his/her image of the world (A.N. Leontiev). Organizing their activity according to the field of meanings, humans thereby continuously confirm its reality. The social space seems so natural, originally rooted to natural properties of objects of nature, that it is noticed usually when one finds oneself within a completely different culture, different way of life.

Just then the difference in the image of the world of people from different cultures is revealed, for example, differences in ethnic self-consciousness, value orientations, stereotypes etc. So, for example, the sociotypical behavior of the person, in which the person and the group act as an entity, neutralizes the tendency for individualization of behavior, growth of its variance, at the same time releasing the person from the burden of choice in typical standard situations. Social stereotypes are like a two-faced Janus. They can appear as individual ways of problem solving by a social group, which reflect individuality of the given community, its peculiarity, as if to look at it from another point of social space, from another culture. The same stereotypes appear as functional-role system qualities for a person within the group, as the sociotypical characteristic of personality, of which the person becomes aware while getting into another culture, like J. Moliere's petty bourgeois in nobility, who only at the end of his life found out that he spoke prose.

While studying the social-historical way of life as a source of personality development it is necessary to take into account the three following characteristics:

First. The category "social-historical way of life" reflects a concrete-historical character for determination of personality development, inalienability of personality development from the evolving social system.

Second. The social-historical way of life represents the potential space of choice, objectively preset to an individual born in one or another society. Namely in this sense, at appearance of the individual in the "human world", he/she already becomes a member of a particular social group in the given society, where both belongingness to the given group, economic conditions and social position, etc., are preset. All of these social-object features for the way of life represent potential possibilities of personality development by one or another life path. They do not automatically define personality development, but are mediated by the following conditions: by the attitudes of the participants of joint activity to types of life activity, social values, norms; by the evaluation of the individual's properties and possibilities (endowments, temperament etc.) by both the participants of joint activity and the person him/herself; by the motives and purposes, for the sake of which a particular person lives. Along the axis of historical time in any social-historical way of life there is an "uncertainty zone" (Yu.M. Lotman), where the subject appears not only as a carrier of sociotypical behavior, but also as individuality. *In sociotypical behavior the subject expresses the acquired patterns of behavior and cognition, superindividual overconscious phenomena, in the manifestation of which he or she acts as an inseparable whole with the social group* [5]; [25]; [51]. In archaic cultures, sociotypical behavior definitely prevails. There exist however, and, in principle, from the viewpoint of the historical-evolutionary approach, must exist norms, which accept the initiative, individual variants of behavior. Especially on the axis of historical time in sociogenesis, individuality in different cultures appeared in objectively conditioned problem-conflict social situations to change one's social status in a group, to prevent a transition to a new age category (initiation ceremonies, kind of exams "for personality"), a transition to a new social group. In these liminal situations a person, as W. Turner put it, has to pass over "the desert of uncertainty", to find his/her own individuality. Thus, in each social-historical way of life in sociogenesis there are mechanisms of "uncertainty elaboration " (Yu.M. Lotman). They provide the appearance of innovations in culture, conveyed by the individuality of a person, that owes the society its origins. Not accidentally in the layers of quite different cultures, for example, in folklore, there are "cock-and-bull stories", "tales", "games", "carnivals" - the school of behavior in untypical situations [28]; [39]; [65]). While investigating the mechanisms of "uncertainty elaboration" in sociogenesis it is necessary to take into account the research of Yu.A. Shreider, devoted to the analysis of evolutionary meaning of nonutilitarian indirect goal setting in the history of culture, and also works treating imagination as an evolutionary mechanism of creation for new worlds creation by a person, testing new paths of development.

Along the axis of social space of personality development, the "zone of uncertainty" is also defined by the social-historical way of life. To illustrate this statement, it is necessary to emphasize the following:

Neither sociological time or the way of life itself, characterized by the historically preset rhythm of change of activity types (game, study, labor, leisure) or by life phases (childhood, youth, maturity, old age), nor anthropological features of the individual themselves do not define the development of a person's individuality. Depending on the social position of a child, preset in the culture, he or she has a different range of possibilities for choice of activities, in which individuality fulfills itself. The more possibilities of choice the subject has, the more obvious it becomes, that the individuality upholds his social position. For example, a child struggles for a certain role in a game, which then defines his or her activity. Considering the relationships between activity and personality in the course of transition from sociogenesis to persogenesis, it is necessary to remember that *activity defines the development of the person's individuality, but the person selects the activity (activities), through which one ascends to maturity.* As far as "leading activities" are concerned, they are not given to the subject, but are rather preset by the particular social situation of development, in which the subject's life proceeds.

"... In the aspect of personality formation it is the activity-mediated type of relationships, established between the child and the group (or person) most referent for him/her in this period rather than a monopoly of particular (leading) activity that is leading at every stage" (Petrovsky A.V. Problem of Personality Development from the Viewpoint of Social Psychology *Questions of Psychology*, 1984. No. 4. p.20.). These relations take shape in the group in which a child can pass the phases of adaptation (mastering social overconscious patterns of social behavior), individualization (an acute search for means and methods of self-realization) and integration of the person in a community (appearance of system qualities of individuality, being potentially able to define the zone of proximal development of the social group). Adaptation, individualization and integration do not make a linear sequence of the person's life in time, but are "mixed lines of evolution" (V.A. Vagner), reflecting the regularities in the historical-evolutionary process of any culture. The contents of each of these phases of the ascent to individuality depends on values, dominating in the social-historical way of life.

Third. The social-historical way of life has a *value-based motive-forming character* expressed in the social program of society's evolution. If there were no risk of terms doubling, one could say that each social-historical way of life has its own "image of value future". Contrary to the anthropocentric paradigm of conceiving human beings, it is not nature itself, not stereotyped values and ideals existing only in form of indifferent "meanings" (A.N. Leontiev), but the activity-mediated type of relationships in the reference group (A.V. Petrovsky) that is the real designer for individual motivation of the person. It depends in many respects on the motive-forming way of life of the reference group, for example, whether the person's behavior will be social or an asocial one.

It is necessary to emphasize especially that *the choice of the leading motivational "life line" in the persogenesis of the person depends in many respects on the particular social-historical way of life.* In the conditions of one

social-historical way of life "the will to power" (A. Adler) can become the
leading motivation of the person, in the conditions of another way of life it can
be the motivation "to be a personality" (A.V. Petrovsky, V.A. Petrovsky), and,
at last, in the situation of epoch fracture and mass identity crises, the
motivation of the "search for meaning" (V. Frankl) begins to claim to play the
role of the leading motivation. In a sense the hypertrophy or monopoly of a
single motivation underlies the shaping of "one-peak" fanatic personality, as
well as the fixation of society on a single "value image of the future" brings
about the occurrence of "one-peak" culture, "monoculture".

Thus, it is shown in the historical-evolutionary approach that introduction
of the category of "social-historical way of life" leads to setting up problems,
the investigation of which allows seeing the regularities of transition from
sociogenesis to persogenesis of the personality. The first of these problems
concerns the study of sociogenetic premises of emergence and evolution of
personality in the history of society on the axe of "historical time". Just setting
up this problem leads investigators to the study of the emergence of the
phenomenon of personality and its importance in the history of social
evolution; to the development of views on the historical character of
seemingly eternal age periodizations - childhood, youth etc.; to the
understanding of the historical determination of the rhythm of change on
different spheres of activity (game, labor, leisure) etc. The second problem is
connected with studying personality development in different cultures of
"social space" of the given epoch, and also in different large and small social
groups of the given culture. An analysis of this problem reveals particular
contents of the functional-role systems qualities of the person, to avoid the
confusion of cultural stereotypes with individual properties and, most
important, to detect the regularities of personality development in the course
of the development of one or another social groups. The greatest contribution
to the solution of this problem is being made by social psychology. New
planes of manifestations of a person's life in different cultures are opened by
ethnopsychological research that has just started to develop. The third
question is connected with the periodization of personality development and
mechanisms of personality development in social groups. This question has
arisen in the social psychology of childhood. In this direction of research the
problems of transition from the social control for regulation of a person's
behavior to self-control, of the transformation of "just known" ideals and
values of the way of life into sense-forming motives of a person's behavior

also rise. These problems are solved on the basis of a study of the mechanisms of interiorization of the social norms in the course of a child's joint activity with adults and peers.

In the study of personality as an element of social system development, the former is defined through its social functions - roles. Describing the role-based sociotypical behavior of a person, sociologists and social psychologists characterize personality as representative of one or another group, profession, nation, class, one or another social entity. Different personal features manifest themselves, depending on what that group is for the person, how much the person is involved in one or another relationships with the group, what do the goals and the problems of the group's joint activity mean for the person. In this connection, to reveal the specificity of the person's manifestations in the group, its contributions to the group's life, it is necessary to reveal the nature of the layer of relationships between the person and the group, to find the system basis, which defines the dynamics and contents of the person's behavior. Intruding into this area of research, psychologists are facing the issues of relationships between social and interpersonal relations, of mechanisms of acquisition of social-historical experience by the person. The adequate setting up the first of these issues presumes giving up the mechanical consideration of interpersonal relations as located "over", "under" or somewhere "outside" social relations, winded by the theories of two factors (see G.M. Andreeva). To analyze how the person is involved into social relations, it is necessary to precisely separate different planes of research of system qualities of personality. So, for example, the study of ideas about relationships between "bosses in general" and "employees in general" in a certain social group - is one plane of studying personality in social relations; research of "norm-role" relationships between the participants of joint activity - represents the second plane; studying relations between people, in which the motives of one person acquire subjective value, personal sense for another, is one more plane for the analysis of system qualities of personality in society development.

To resolve the issue of the relationship between the social and interpersonal relations it seems reasonable to single out three levels of analysis of systems qualities of personality in social relations: quasi-psychological, inter-psychological and intra-psychological ones, that outline a picture of the transition from sociogenesis to persogenesis of personality. At the *quasi-psychological* level, the object of research is social roles, perception stereotypes, personality traits represented in notions, that reflect some personality type characteristic of the given culture, nation or group. At this level most of the research on the problem of the social-typical in personality is carried out, in particular, research on the social and national character. It is worth mentioning that some widespread questionnaires, like 16PF, belong to the inventories, working primarily at the quasi-psychological level of personality analysis. The conceptual bridge between quasi-psychological and inter-psychological levels of personality analysis has been built on the concept of dispositional regulation of the social behavior of persons elaborated by V.A. Yadov (1980). This concept can form the basis for the development of typologies of social characters. At the same time, this concept makes it possible to investigate first of all the representations of norms, values, ideals, which function as "just known" motives of person's behavior. In order to approach "really functioning" motives, it is necessary to address the inter-psychological level of analysis of the person's relationships in the society.

At the inter-psychological level of analysis, research of person's social relations, mediated by joint activity is carried out. Thus, within the framework of the theory of activity mediation of interpersonal relations of A.V. Petrovsky (1979), a number of phenomena (for example, collectivistic self-determination, reference) have been obtained, which at the same time characterize a group and a person's qualities. The question arises, under which conditions these phenomena, describing first of all *normatively preset role relationships* between the participants of a joint activity, turn into another class of phenomena, reflecting *personal-sense* relationships between people? The conditions of the transition from the phenomena of "group - person" to sense manifestations of the personality can be investigated based on the material of social perception. Thus, phenomena of interpersonal perception as conditioned by different sets, experimentally revealed by A.A. Bodalev (1965), characterize the norm-role perception of a person as a typical representative of one or another social group; they can be used as a sort of indicator of the level of relationships, into which the person is involved. If a person declines from the patterns, which represent the norm in the eyes of persons communicating with him/her, from various standards and stereotypes, then the conditions emerge for the transition from the "object type" perception to the "subject type" one (A.U. Kharash), from normatively preset role relationships to personality-sense relationships. *The deviation from the normatively preset activity is a condition of the transition from role relationships to sense relationships of the person*, which are investigated at the *intra-psychological level* of analysis of a person's relation in the society [1].

The second big problem which arises during the analysis of the transition from sociogenesis to persogenesis of personality, is the problem of the mechanism of transformation of "social situation for development" into intra-psychological personality manifestations. With all the diversity of interpretations of the process of socialization there are no meaningful alternatives to its understanding as the transition from inter-psychological to intra-psychological offered by L.S. Vygotsky. This transition is based on the mechanism of interiorization - exteriorization. In the mechanism of socialization one should single out three different facets: *individualization* - the transition from social collective activity to individual forms of activity; *intimization* - the transition from "we" to "me", that reflects the process of formation of self-consciousness of the person; *construction of the internal plane of consciousness* - the transformation of the external to the internal [21].

In the historical-evolutionary approach it is argued, that the initial "cells" in the transition from sociogenesis to persogenesis of personality are originally joint acts of behavior, *assistance*, transforming the social situation of personality development, rather than individual, absorbing effects of the social environment. *Assistance is the initial moment of persogenesis of personality, generation of a "sense image of the world".*

In Russian psychology, the process of child personality development from real assistance along with a socioculture sample with adults and peers to self-control over one's own actions has been investigated in detail in research of A.V. Zaporozhets and his colleagues. It has been shown in this research that in the course of co-actions with an adult, a child transforms functional-role relationships in a group, providing only known neutral motives of actions, that are corrected by late emotions, into personal-sense relationships, induced by sense-forming motives of actions, that are corrected by anticipative emotions. Thus, in the social space of the way of life of a certain culture, the process of transition from sociogenesis to persogenesis of the person moves from the "assistance" as initial cells of personality development, to the self-control of behavior, induced by the sense-forming motives of the personality.

Thus, depending on the problem facing the researcher, three different facets of interiorization as the mechanism of socialization show through - individualization, intimization and construction of the internal plane of consciousness. Disregarding these aspects of interiorization, it would be hardly possible to penetrate into the mental nature for mechanisms of communication, learning and personality upbringing, to reveal the regularities of a person's acquisition of social-historical experience. However, with a deeper penetration into the essence of these mechanisms, the abstraction, seeing the personality mainly in the context of sociogenesis, essentially loses its influence. Being quite pertinent and even necessary on the quasi-psychological and inter-psychological levels of investigating personality in the social system, this abstraction gets into an obvious contradiction with the facts as soon as the investigator addresses the process of persogenesis - the study of the moving forces of personality development and its life span, i.e., the path where a person becomes not only the subject of his/her own development, but also the master of his/her fate.

CHAPTER 6

PERSONALITY SELF-FULFILLMENT AS A CONDITION AND THE PURPOSE OF THE HISTORICAL-EVOLUTIONARY DEVELOPMENT OF SOCIETY

In the historical-evolutionary approach to the psychology of personality it is stated that the persogenesis of personality occurs simultaneously as though in two regimes: the regime of "joining the social-historical experience of the society" and the regime of "transformation and reproduction" of both acquired social-historical experience, and various individual properties of the person (temperament, potential, functional psychophysiological systems forming during one's life, that underlie the subject activity). A person, making contributions into sociogenesis, enriches human history, the necessary condition and purpose of which is the development of human individuality. In general, individuality appears in the form of attitudes, generated in the course of the person's life in society in case of some necessary anthropogenetic premises, that provide orientation in the hierarchy of values and mastering one's behavior in a situation of struggle of motives. They are embodied through activity and communication in the products of culture, in other people, and in oneself for the sake of continuation of the way of life valuable for the given person.

This understanding of individuality is based first of all on the *principle of growth of the variability of system elements as the criterion of progressive evolution*, described above, and also on the concept of sense formation of personality developed within the activity theory approach [1]; [2]; [14]; [15]; [29]. The historical-evolutionary approach and concept of sense formation of personality provide an outline of a solution for the following three problems:

General characterization of the psychology of individuality and its place in the psychology of personality;

Revealing features for the units of analysis of the dynamic organization of the personality on the basis of research of the phenomenon for sense attitudes of the person;

Developing views on the psychological mechanisms of "personality self-transcendence" (S.L. Rubinstein), that provide self-fulfillment of the person in his/her life course.

Despite many attempts to study the problem of individuality using such approaches in psychology as "understanding psychology", individual psychology, humanistic psychology, personology, existential psychology, the research in persogenesis remains so far "terra incognita" and simultaneously "blue bird" for the psychologists of quite different schools and backgrounds. Perhaps the inertia of classical rational thinking, described in the first chapter, has never appeared more strongly than in the psychology of individuality. The psychology of individuality was separated from the general psychology of personality, character was identified with personality, abilities were cut off from will, the will was correlated with the constitution type, and then the individuality of personality was "cut out" from all of these, without any beforehand selected fashion. In the activity theory approach to personality, attempts are persistently undertaken to bring the problem of individuality nearer (K.A. Abulkhanova-Slavskaya, B.S. Bratus, F.E. Vasilyuk, V.K. Viliunas, V.A. Ivannikov, V.F. Petrenko, V.A. Petrovsky, V.V. Stolin, V.I. Slobodchikov, A.G. Shmelev). Due to this research, two planes of studying the individuality of personality as the subject of activity can be singled out: productive and instrumental ones.

Productive manifestations of personality as the subject of activity cover the processes of activity of the person, deviating from normatively prescribed lines of behavior, namely the processes of self-devotion, transformation of oneself or others. In the case where such a deviation happens, the person collides with the problem of choice between different motives and roles in an uncertain situation. It is the situations of free choice where the person especially vividly manifests him/herself as the subject of activity, *and the history of personality development in persogenesis becomes the history of alternatives rejected by the person* (B.F. Porshnev). Any typology of personality as individuality, any periodization of mature personality development, which is yet to be created, cannot keep aside specific manifestations of personality in the situation of choice, analysis of the person's orientation in the system of sense-forming motives. Not accidentally P.Y. Galperin (1976) noted that the main criterion of maturity of the person is his/her responsibility for his/her actions, and it is a socially responsible subject that can be considered as personality in the full sense of the word. In a situation of choice the person has to create ways and means for mastering his/her behavior. The instrumental historical-genetic method of research of higher mental functions (L.S. Vygotsky, A.R. Luria) is able to bring the psychological analysis of the problem of choice from the sphere of speculative reasoning into the sphere of experimental research. The search for external and internal means in the situation of the struggle of motives, research of rudimentary cultural forms of will, like casting lots, opens the way to studying the origin of different defense mechanisms of personality. These devices of self-defense and compensation are considered in L.S. Vygotsky's school as a means of self-regulation, mastering the person's behavior, rather than an opposition to consciousness (B.V. Zeigarnik). The magic actions of exortion of malicious spirits - aren't they rudimentary forms of catharsis in sociogenesis? Identification - is it not an action of substitution of another person by oneself, reduced and transferred into the ideal plane in ontogenesis? All these questions require special research, directed at studying social genesis of self-defense in the history of society and persogenesis.

Personality as the subject of activity shows up also in the processes of shaping new goals, goal-setting (O.K. Tikhomirov). Productive manifestations of personality as the subject of activity include not only transformation of oneself, but also transformations, which the person brings into the sense sphere of other people, into culture, into public production through his/her deeds and actions. In the conception of "personality contributions", developed by A.V. Petrovsky and V.A. Petrovsky (1982) it is emphasized that activity of the person, that implements his/her sense attitudes to people, is carried out by deeds, i.e., unintended, not normatively prescribed manifestations of the subject's activity, transforming other people and, thereby, making significant contribution to them. In these, deed personalization of the person, that is, his/her continuation in other people occurs. One's actualization in others, rather than "self-actualization", as described by A. Maslow and G. Allport, represents the way of individuality development. Thus, the creative nature of the person as the subject of activity, of the individuality shows in the processes of personal choice, new goal setting, in mastering critical situations, and in transforming other people and oneself.

Instrumental manifestations of personality as the subject of activity include character and abilities. Abilities define the measure of success and efficiency of activity, as psychologists holding quite different opinions on their genesis (A.N. Leontiev, S.L. Rubinstein, B.M. Teplov) concordantly note. *Character as an instrumental manifestation of personality is understood as a fixed form of expression of sense experience, sense attitudes, that become actualized in the person's individual style of acting, through which one or another motives are realized. If motivational lines define the strategy of the person's life, the character defines the tactics of behavior of the person, pursuing the achievement of his/her motives.* Such an understanding of character is based on the ideas, developed by L.S. Vygotsky, S.L. Rubinstein and D.N. Uznadze. According to these authors, holding dynamic conceptions of character, the units for analysis of character are the dynamic tendencies of personality, generalized attitudes of the person. These attitudes have some peculiarities. First, sense attitudes keep in time, conserve in themselves the leading relations of the person to the reality, thus providing stability of the person's behavior. Second, these attitudes become actualized at meeting an appropriate situation and show in the individual style of activity of the person. Third, the fate of the attitudes in activity allows understanding the genesis of character (S.L. Rubinstein), namely, sense attitudes become character traits. Fourth, sense attitudes manifest themselves in psychotonic activity of the person (the material substratum of character). Attempts to investigate the latter were undertaken by A.V. Zaporozhets and A. Wallon. Postural-tonic expressions of the character are the visible language of nonverbal communication. Leaning upon these manifestations is one of the ways to transform the character, to reconstruct it in the processes of communication and activity. Often the situations of struggle between personality and character emerge. Personality relates to character as something external, helping or hindering the achievement of its purposes. Very often we meet people, who complain about their character, but it is hardly possible to find someone, who would complain about his or her personality. Such relations between the content plane of personality (values, senses, motives) and the expression plane of personality (character) provide unambiguous evidence for unity, but not identity of personality and character.

The initial stimulus for the conceptualization of the psychology of individuality, described above, has become the research of sense attitudes as units of the dynamic organization of personality [1]. In this regard it is necessary to single out general peculiarities of sense attitudes, the study of which has become the starting point of the search for a special "supersensory object-related" reality - the sense world of individuality:

> sense attitude, being an embodiment of personal sense in the form of readiness for some activity with certain direction, stabilizes the process of activity as a whole, gives a stability to the activity. This function can directly show up in the general sense of coloring of different actions, included in the structure of activity, in "superfluous" movements, sense-based slips and clauses;
>
> phenomenologically sense attitudes manifest themselves in seemingly casual, unmotivated "deviations" from the normative behavior for the given situation (for example, slips, name confusion etc.);
>
> independence of sense attitudes from their awareness (the subject can be aware of some personal sense, but the awareness is not enough for changing it);
>
> impossibility of its direct incorporation in "meanings", of its "formalization" (F.V. Bassin);
>
> the shift of sense attitudes is always mediated by the change of the subject's activity and his/her social position. This is the essential difference of sense attitude and personal sense that it expresses in activity from and various subjective formations like "relations" (V.N. Myasischev), fixed social attitudes, "significant experiences" (F.V. Bassin), etc., that can be changed directly under the influence of verbal information.

The above-described peculiarity of sense attitudes is necessary to take into account during an analysis of such a practical and vital problem as the problem of upbringing a person. The psychological object of upbringing is the sense sphere of personality, the system of personal senses and sense attitudes that realize the former in activity. It follows from such an understanding of the psychological object of upbringing that re-education of the person always goes through a change of activity, and thereby through the change of sense attitudes; it basically cannot be attained by means of purely verbal influences. Only the sets of goal and operational levels are subject to direct influences of various instructions. The ways of change for sense attitudes and the sets of lower levels radically differ: sense attitudes of the person *are re-educated*, while goal and operational sets *are relearned*.

On the basis of *the principle of activity mediation of sense attitudes of the person,* a cycle of applied research, dealing with problems of choice of motives in simulation games, upbringing, criminal behavior and social-psychological rehabilitation of personality has been carried out [15]; [17]; [31]; [44]; [62]; [72].

When reviewing retrospectively different lines of the movement toward understanding of peculiarities of the sense nature of individuality, it becomes obvious, that the term "sense formation of personality" has played the role of symbol, which reflected an attempt of a number of researchers to reach the special supersensory object-related reality of the "subjective" world of the person [14]. And it is not accidentally, that the attempt to construe the object of the psychology of personality based on the notion "sense formation of personality" lacking a precise ontological status, has been subjected to thorough criticism (see [23]). So, for example, V.P. Zinchenko noted that "sense formations" are "imaginary essences", and the unit of the personality is an act. A.M. Matiushkin has cast doubt on the statement that an analysis of deviations from the normatively prescribed lines of behavior is an adequate method of studying sense manifestations of individuality. Such a criticism of the conception of sense formations of personality had its reasons. However, time has shown that the research of "imaginary essences" like sense formations of personality, has played an important role in the psychology of personality and has led many researchers, whether they are aware of it or not, to liberation from the fetters of classical rational thinking. Ignorance of the supersensory subjective world of individuality by the latter, V.K. Viliunas, precisely named the most absurd scientific error of the twentieth century. The discussions emerging around the conception of sense formations make it possible to specify ideas about the nature of sense formations and to sketch the perspectives of their further investigation in present-day psychology.

First of all, the timid characteristic of the phenomena of sense attitudes of the person and, later on, sense formations of personality as a whole in terms of "deviations", "distortions" of the normatively prescribed lines of social behavior is nothing but a tribute to classical rational thinking [1]. Looking at the manifestations of sense attitudes through the prism of "correct" rational action, you interpret them as "deviations" from social reality. Actually, it seems quite reasonable to assume that there are supersensory "object-related" (A.N. Leontiev) "sense worlds of individuality" opening behind the rich phenomenology of "deviations". Figuratively speaking, the world of "social norms" occupies the same place on the continuum of "sense worlds of individuality", as the world of classical physics on the continuum of worlds of relativistic physics. Could, for example, the phenomenon of "idealization" of the beloved person be called "deviation"? The lay consciousness sees just such an "error", "delusion", "decoration" in this phenomenon. The psychological truth is that the phenomenon of "idealization" of the beloved person belongs to the phenomena of "object-relatedness", lying in the special "sense" dimension of reality designated in the activity theory approach (A.N. Leontiev).

In the study of the object-relatedness phenomena many questions arise, among which a special place is occupied by the issue of the genesis of object-relatedness. In the most preliminary form we can assume that the object-relatedness passes the three following stages in its development: in phylogenesis the world shows up for animals as *bio-sense space*, space of biological senses; at early stages of development of humankind the world appears for a person as *space of meanings* (this is especially vividly seen using the example of analysis of archaic consciousness, where sense and meaning are still inseparable). And, at last, the next stage of the development of object-relatedness is the birth of *personal sense space*. Various phenomena of individuality, perceived as "deviations", including the phenomenon of "idealization" of the beloved person [22] refer just to the manifestations of the personal sense space. The nature of this non-symbolical personal sense space has been rather precisely described by M.K. Mamardashvilli, discussing M. Proust's character: this character presents a necklace to a woman, bearing an image of the world where she is the most clever and beautiful in the world. Immediately he hears the words of prostitutes spoken to this woman, bearing the image of the social habitual world in which she agrees to have sex for 20 francs. M.K. Mamardashvilli makes the following comments on this situation: *"The necklace is presented not to the loved women, but loved is the women to whom a necklace is presented. It ... is the theme of things, which bear senses.*

You see, the necklace is the thing. In regular psychology a thing serves as a mediating link of human feelings, clear as they are. Say, I love someone and as a sign of my love, I present them with a necklace. In this sense the necklace is a sign... And it can be replaced by another sign. The sign by its nature can be replaced by any other sign, if we agree ... And we deal with the non-symbolical theory of things... Here the necklace is irreplaceable: it symbolizes the woman that is loved. First, it is not a sign, and second, the feeling here is not clear by itself, transparent for oneself, it was constructed *not by way of choice and thinking, but by a completely different special way* (italics mine - A.A.)" (M.K. Mamardashvilli. *Lectures on Proust: The Psychological Topology of the Way*. M., 1995, p.32).

The symptom of "non-transferability" of the sense world into the sign world of the culture described in the above-mentioned example has a principal significance for the understanding of perspectives of the sense conception of individuality. It follows from this example, first, that semiotic approaches, suffering from natural lingvocentrism, including the semiotic concept of culture by Yu.M. Lotman obviously do not suffice for the elaboration of the concept of personal-sense space. Highly heuristic as it is, the semiotic concept of culture highlights only one layer of the special dimension of reality - the layer of "semiosphere" (Yu.M. Lotman), which, in spite of its importance for the history of humankind, does not exhaust all the variety of worlds constructed in sociogenesis. Unlike the semiotic conception of culture, the historical-evolutionary activity theory approach tries to find ways to penetrate into the personal-sense space, existing together with the space of object-related meanings, and to reveal mutual transitions between these facets of the object-related world of humankind [6]; [29]; [44]; [72].

Secondly, in an analysis of the sense world given by M.K. Mamardashvilli, the existence of quite special methods for work of constructing personal-sense space was vividly demonstrated. In due course, A.N. Leontiev characterized a similar kind of special activity of personal sense production as an "internal work", in which the solution of "sense tasks" does occur. At the same time A.N. Leontiev and S.L. Rubinstein, while analyzing the psychological nature of such an essential characteristic of individuality as "self-transcendence", have paid the most attention to different aspects of the origin of the sense world, almost leaving aside the basic question: "Where does the subject come, when he/she transcends oneself? In what way and in which products does persogenesis return to sociogenesis?"

Reflection on this problem in the framework of the historical-evolutionary approach allows us to single out two poles of research of the movement from persogenesis to sociogenesis, from the intrapsychological to the interpsychological, from interiorization to exteriorization: the pole of sense creation and the pole of sense embodiment. In psychology original research has been performed in recent years which can be referred to as the pole of "sense creation". Among them one should mention first of all the conceptualization of the special activity of experiencing (F.E. Vasilyuk) and the research on the construction of sense in volitional action (V.A. Ivannikov). The "psychology of subjectness" dealing with the problem of ideal representation of the person in other people (V.A. Petrovsky) takes a sort of intermediate position between these two poles. On the conjunction of the historical-evolutionary approach and the psychology of subjectivity, an attempt was undertaken to reveal the concrete psychological mechanism underlying the subject's self-transcendence. *The mechanism, providing the "small" dynamics of personality development, is the interplay between sense attitudes of personality, expressing the tendency toward stability, and transsituational activity, expressing the tendency toward change: if the attitudes try to keep the subject's activity in preset limits, transsituational activity breaks through these attitudes and brings the person to other levels for the solution of these problems* [13]; [14]. A.V. Petrovsky and M.G. Yaroshevsky (1996), describing this mechanism of movement of personality noted, that the person in the course of solving his/her vital problems makes transitions from one temporary stability to another temporary stability in the process of his/her development.

The second pole was made by research on the crystallization of senses in the world of human culture, occurring in the course of persogenesis returning to sociogenesis, i.e., in a sort of "world-making", being a result of the subject's self-transcendence. To see the perspective of the research of persogenesis returning to sociogenesis, the following analogy from the history of discovery of object-relatedness phenomena is helpful. Once in the field of psychology of thinking, M. Wertheimer and K. Dunker referred to the phenomenon of functional fixation as one of the brightest pieces of evidence for the existence of the phenomenological field. Afterwards, research of a similar layer of phenomena led N.A. Bernshtein, A.N. Leontiev and P.Ya. Galperin to the idea of the existence of the "field of object meanings", and the phenomenon of functional fixation was placed by them to the class of object-relatedness phenomena. In the research of the motivational sphere of personality, K. Lewin offered his fundamental ideas about the "demanding character" of things and about "life space", that stimulated an understanding of motive as an object of a need in the beginning of the thirties (A.N. Leontiev), and the idea of "motivational field" of the person still later (V.K. Viliunas). In the same historical context, the historical-evolutionary approach in the psychology of personality, growing up on the basis of culture-historical psychology and activity theory approach in general psychology, must meet new phenomenological sociology, raising the problem of *social construction of reality* (P. Berger, T. Luckmann) and addressing the analysis of *sense structure of the social world* (D. Worsh, D. Silverman, P. Filmer). Such a meeting would help to understand how the history of development of a changing person in a changing world is being transformed into the history of development of the sense social world, and the psychology of personality is being transformed into a constructive science of history-making human being.

CHAPTER 7

PRACTICAL PSYCHOLOGY AS A FACTOR OF DESIGNING THE EDUCATIONAL FIELD OF PERSONALITY

The leitmotiv of the final period of development of the historical-evolutionary approach in the psychology of personality was a dream that on the threshold of the 21st century psychology in social practice might become a constructive factor of the evolution of society. First of all, this dream was cast by the idea of V.I. Vernadsky about the personal root of the noosphere, an idea that has been laconically and precisely conveyed by M.G. Yaroshevsky as follows: "Vernadsky linked the acceleration of progress with the energy and activity of persons, possessing these ways [ways of discovering new scientific truths - A.A.]. One should, however, remember that, taking into account his "cosmic" way of understanding the universe, progress was considered as the development of the noosphere, through the change of biosphere and, therefore, of the whole planet as a systems entity, rather than as the development of knowledge as such. *The psychology of personality appeared to be a sort of "energetic" essence due to which the evolution of the entity Earth as a cosmic whole goes on"* [italics mine - A.A.]. (M.G. Yaroshevsky. *Historical psychology of science*. St.-Petersburg. 1995, pp. 335-336). For this dream to come true the following problems have been set up and mostly solved:

Designing practical psychology as the basis for social reformation of the education sphere;

Validation of views about education as the mechanism of sociogenesis

supporting or eliminating manifestations of individuality in the
historical-evolutionary process;

Development of the strategy of reforming the education system,
promoting the transition from a adaptive paradigm of "knowledge,
skills, habits" - to a paradigm of "developing education";

Realization of L.S. Vygotsky's idea of a methodological potential of
practical psychology as a condition for overcoming the crisis in
psychology;

Change of social status of practical psychology in the education system as
a sphere of the social practice ([6]; [7]; [8]; [9]; [58]; [59]; [60]; [64];
[65]; [67]; [68]; [69]; [73]).

*From reformation of the pedagogical method - to the reformation of
social organization of life in the education system.* In the historical-
evolutionary approach education is considered as a mechanism of
sociogenesis supporting or eliminating manifestation of individuality in a
social system. In totalitarian cultures of usefulness, the forms of education
prevail that are based on standard average level programs as well as on the
social standard "to be like everyone else". Just through education the
totalitarian culture of usefulness sharpens the mechanisms of social control,
that aim to provide the leveling of personality, the shaping of the "social
character" (E. Fromm), which would fit the needs of the totalitarian culture. In
other words, in the cultures of usefulness the sociogenetic mechanism of
education is designed in order to suppress any deviations from the normative
sociotypical behavior. An ideal of a pupil in such cultures is a so-called
"average pupil." In the cultures of dignity, with their main objective "to live,
rather than to survive", education supports the variability of persons, prepares
a person for solving non-standard rather than just typical life problems. In
fact, in social systems the tendencies both toward preservation and toward
change of the systems are simultaneously realized through education. The
point is to find such an optimum combination of these tendencies which can
provide a national standard of education inherent in the given civilization, and
at the same time open the most possibilities for personality development.

Those people who feel responsible for the development of the education
system in society, as a rule, face the following alternative: either to become a
conductor of the culture of usefulness and through education to shape unified
persons – a business that resembles in a sense the factory of *comprachicos*

described by V. Hugo (*The man who laughs*), or to start construing in the territory of education such a way for organization of life that would help each person to find him/herself. The choice made in this situation determines the place and the mission of education in the society: *in the first case education lags behind the society, in the second case it provides for the development of the society. This choice determines the direction of education reforms.* The real reform of education is, first of all, the reform of the entire life of the growing and learning child, not only or primarily a reform of the pedagogical method, one or another special educational technology.

The changes occurring in Russia have been given a chance to create such an educational system, centered around the problem of enhancing the possibilities for a competent choice of one's way of life by each person. Growing variability of life forms, increasing freedom of personal choice, weakening of traditional knowledge transmission systems due to the changes of value orientations in the generation of "children" as compared to the generation of "adults" in a dynamic unstable period of Russian history have become the objective social premises for the appearance of variable education.

From federal sociocultural programs "unordinary children in unordinary world" - to practical psychology and variable developing meaning-related education. Aiming at the transition from the adaptive-disciplinary model of unified education to the person-oriented child-centered model of variable education, the following programs have been elaborated: "Creative portential", "Social-psychological support, education and upbringing of children with abnormal development" and "Social support service for children and youth".

These programs were intended for the solution of several tasks. First, they historically proceeded directly from L.S. Vygotsky's pedological cultural-historical views and from that led to the revival of the child-centered individual approach inherent in pedology. Second, in the social plane these programs helped to shake the myth of "equality" of all children based on the political party-class principles of selection of children in educational institutions. The myth of equality of all children was one of the political barriers on the way to variable education and a cause for exile of pedology into an "intellectual GULAG". Third, these programs created in society an objective need for a psychological service in education, aimed at prophylactic, diagnostic, developing, correction and rehabilitation work with personality. For the faceless totalitarian educational system that adjusts a child to the curriculum, instead of creating a program that would consider the child's motivation and abilities, the psychologist is persona non grata. A psychological service is appropriate and necessary first of all in the system of variable education, opening a range of possibilities for individual development of the person in the world of culture.

Gifted children, abnormal children and children with deviant behavior represent sharp corners of a triangle, representing zones of risk, zones of special attention for the educational system. The development of the abovementioned programs, often associated with the "triangle of disturbance of totalitarian depersonalized education", in many aspects stimulated the transition to active elaboration of variable education in different areas of the educational space in Russia.

As a result of the development of the program complex "Unordinary children in an unordinary world" the model of unified education has been shaken. In the course of realization of these programs the concept of "education" itself, the objective of education, the place of developing pedagogy in the system of variable education have been reconsidered. A need for practical psychology that became the core of variable education, emerged in the culture.

Variable education is the educational testing of other uncommon ways of resolving various indeterminate situations in a culture and providing the person with a range of possibilities to choose one's own destiny. In contrast the alternative education, *variable education not only substitutes the common educational norms with antinorms, but helps the person to find other ways of comprehension and experiencing of knowledge in a changing world. Variable education is understood as a process directed towards extension of possibilities for the competent choice of one's own life course by the person and towards the person's self-development. The objective of variable education is creating in joint activity with adults and peers such a picture of the world which would provide the person's orientation in various kinds of life situations, including indeterminate situations. In the course of variable education a child enters the culture, e.g. masters the ways of thinking and abilities with which people have been building human civilization for many centuries.*

The pedagogy of development with inherent child-centeredness and goal orientation for mastering the ways of thinking in a given society and in the history of humankind that is taking shape within the educational system, is the foundation for the search of a system of innovation technologies, expanding the possibilities of personality development. The search strategy for these technologies is the strategy of construing the developing way of life, different kinds of educating and upbringing environments.

In general, the pedagogy of development is based on the methodology of practical psychology, which embodied in the ideology of present-day Russian education the ideas of cultural-historical psychology, the general psychological activity theory approach and the historical-evolutionary approach.

Value orientations of the practical psychology of education. In the treasury of the ideas of the practical psychology of education the following value orientations should be considered in the construction of the strategy for educational reform: from selective assessment - to the diagnostics of development; from the adaptive-disciplinary model of knowledge and skill acquisition - to the birth of a picture of the world in joint activity with adults and peers; from information-based cognitive pedagogy - to meaning-related value-based pedagogy; from the technology of education according to the formula "answers without questions" - to life tasks and child's cognitive motivation; from the child's "learned helplessness" - to oversituational activity and setting up supergoals; from the lesson as authoritarian monologue - to the lesson as collaboration and co-creation; from the language of administrative "commands" - to the language of "agreements" and "recommendations"; from school-centeredness to child-centeredness and, at last, from the culture of usefulness - to the culture of dignity. This spectrum of positions, explicated here in deliberately expressive form and is embodied through courses of teachers' advanced training as practical psychologists. It was created all over the country, in mass media, administrative directives as algorithms of activity for large social groups, developing programs for preschool, facultative and general education, and helped to create the ideology of developing variable meaning-related education based on practical psychology. Just these value orientations, penetrating into public opinion in the sphere of education, helped to build an education that is able, as L.S. Vygotsky put it, to pass from impersonal systems to the destiny of every single person. At the same time, practical psychology as a methodology of education is just the beginning, rather than the end of the way from the culture of usefulness to the culture of dignity, the way not yet passed. An important milestone on the way became the system of strategic orientations for variable education.

METHODOLOGICAL ORIENTATIONS OF DEVELOPMENT OF VARIABLE EDUCATION

First. *From separate alternative scientific pedagogical schools - to the system of variable innovative technologies in the context of cultural-historical pedagogy of development.* An important role in the development of variable education belongs to "author schools". Essentially, author schools are the mechanisms of search, testing different ways of education in the culture. In spite of the diversity of innovative author schools, they can be subdivided into two types: instrumental and culturologic schools. The focus of attention of the instrumental schools is, as a rule, one or another specific pedagogical method found in practical activity due to the talent of the innovative teacher. This method as a tool of pedagogical labor can be mastered and included both in the traditional educational system, and in the developmental pedagogy.

Culturological author schools, in the broad sense of the word, have different origins. They have originated, as a rule, at the junction between world view concepts and innovative technologies. For example, Waldorf pedagogy stems from R. Steiner's philosophy. It is especially important to pay attention to culturologic author schools like: "Didactic system of education by L.V. Zankov", "System of developing education by D.B. Elkonin-V.V. Davydov", the program "Development" by A.V. Zaporozhets - L.A. Venger," Activity theory of education by P.Ya. Galperin - N.F. Talyzina", "School of the dialogue of cultures" of V.S. Bibler.

The entire spectrum of the enumerated innovative directions in pedagogical thinking has its roots in the cultural-historical psychology and activity theory approach of L.S. Vygotsky and A.N. Leontiev and the methodology of humanitarian knowledge of M.M. Bakhtin. All these approaches overcome the science-practice parallelism that existed for many years: theory separately, technology separately.

In that regard one of the important tasks while analyzing the future of variable education is the synthesis of these approaches in the context of the system of pedagogy of development, that would maintain the unique face of each of these author schools.

For these purposes a scientific-methodical center "DAD" (Diagnostics. Adaptation. Development), named after L.S. Vygotsky, and a scientific-methodical center "Developmental Pedagogy", named after L.V. Zankov, have been organized. A center of medical pedagogy, that could reasonably bear A.R. Luria's name, is actively functioning in Moscow.

Second. *From the monopoly of state education - to the coexistence and cooperation of state, private and family education.* In the evolution of education in the social-historical process the combination of state, private and family education is the optimum range of possibilities for the individual development of personality (projects: Standard regulations of family education, Standard regulations for general educational institutions in the Russian Federation, Standard regulations of external studies).

Third. *From "a-national" unitarian school - to ethnic differentiation of education in the system of the general educational space of Russia.* The national school is one of the important elements of keeping and developing of the unique "Ego", the spiritual kernel of an ethnic community. In this connection, the mastering of the native languages by the ethnic community representatives is extremely important, not only as a means of communication, but also as the means of entering the ethnic culture. A system of further education has large resources for personality development through joining national customs and traditions.

Fourth. *From subject-centeredness - to educational fields in building curricula for general educational institutions.* The transition from building curricula from special subjects - to educational fields such as "social disciplines", "natural disciplines" etc., opens first of all the possibility of creating variants of curricula depending on regional and national features, to increase variability of the contents of education in general. This is an important but not the only resource of variability that originated due to the transition from subject-centered education to educational fields. Opening the possibility of interdisciplinary transitions between different subjects, hitherto separated, is another resource of variability following from the given strategy, that it has not yet been realized sufficiently.

Earlier the "cuckoo" principle dominated in traditional education: each new subject - like information, law, or economy - tried to throw other subjects out from the nest of school knowledge. At the transition from subject-centered education to educational fields, increasing variability becomes an important condition for the birth of new courses giving a holistic, rather than mosaic, picture of the world. Thus, the transition from subject-centered education to educational fields stimulates the appearance of integrative educational courses providing the pupils' acquisition of an entire picture of the world.

Fifth. *From the "straight" development of educational institutions - to the "mixed" lines of development of educational institutions.* It seemed evident only recently that evolution takes place in society only along "straight" lines of different types of educational institutions. In a preschool institution there was one world and at school - another, in institutions of further education there was a third world, in professional school - one more, and, at last, in a college there was an absolutely special world. In other words, rigid boundaries existed not only between the states, but also between independent types of educational institutions. At the same time, all the experience of evolution in nature and culture shows that "straight" evolution inevitably causes recourse and impedes the growth of diverse life forms. Biological and social organisms, with functioning programs rigidly tied to standard stable life conditions, die out especially quickly (V.A. Vagner).

On the dynamic phase of social life, the evolution on "mixed" lines inevitably begins to prevail. This stimulates a rapid process of combining school with kindergarten (complex "school - kindergarten"), and middle schools with high school (complex "middle school - high school"), challenging petrified typical rules, that regulate scholarly life, together with the appearance of colleges, technical Lyceums, etc. Special interest is directed at various sorts of schools in the system of further education, the unique system where child comes him/herself, driven by his/her interests, motivated by knowledge and creativity.

The evolution of educational institutions along "mixed" lines makes the educational system of Russia more flexible and tolerant to different changes. It allows the developing child to fulfill oneself without conflicts in the world of continuous variable education, rather than being an eternal migrant running from one alien territory to another. The formula "a task gives birth to an organ" (N.A. Bernstein) is a law of any evolution and hence it is normal when the tasks of the development of society at a dynamic phase of its history bring such a differentiation of education, which provides an integration of educational fields.

For these mixed institutions, the legal language of statutes, instructive letters, contracts is more adequate than that of standard regulations. Therefore an attempt to lead Lyceums, gymnasiums, colleges and school-laboratories into the trap of standard regulations, e.g., to put an identical strait-jacket on the new kinds of educational institutions, that are not yet aware of themselves, is hardly justified.

Sixth. *From a monopolist textbook - to variable textbooks.* The dynamics of increasing options to choose among textbooks in 1990-1996 is an eloquent illustration of the transition of Russia from the traditional to the variable education. A breakthrough in the renewal of contents of textbooks can be anticipated at least in two directions. The first direction is the so-called "motivating textbooks" in the system of further education. The main task of this series of textbooks is to "wake up" an interest, a cognitive motivation in the child, to shape the wish to learn. The second direction of the breakthrough is the creation of textbooks in metadisciplines, through disciplines. New metadisciplines, including ecology, law and economy, though at the first sight may seen paradoxical, are more open to the ideas of cultural-historical pedagogy of development. In these disciplines, the authors and the teachers, who came from research institutes and universities and did not receive the training of traditional information pedagogy in pedagogical colleges, more boldly introduce, for example, the cultural-functional approach to the economy into high school. It is rather symbolic that the positions of this new generation of teachers coincide in many aspects with these of F.F. Zelinsky, who was a fervent fighter for teaching ancient cultures at school. F.F. Zelinsky defended the idea that gymnasium education by its spirit is incompatible with narrow professional training and leads to deeper layers of culture, rather than special knowledge. The tasks of gymnasium education are to raise a Cultural Person who, through studying ancient culture at school, develops an "enhanced Ego", becomes a Citizen of Europe. An economic and ecological education helps the growing person to become a citizen of Earth as our Common Home.

Seventh. *From monofunctional technical means of education - to multifunctional means and information technologies.* There is a gradual change of technical education means by their function and place in the educational process: from visual-demonstration - to teaching means, from separate allowances and instruments - to microlaboratories. The special place is more and more obviously taken by information technologies that become not just simple training tools, but teach a pupil to live in the information environment, introduce the pupils into the information culture. Thereby, information technologies by their cultural-psychological function, solve such a task of variable education as the pupil's involvement in the global cultural and educational space of our changing world.

* * *

The described strategic orientations of variable education open the possibility of designing education as a mechanism of sociogenesis directed at the development of individuality of the person. The realization of these orientations in the sphere of education as a social practice allowed taking a step toward changing the social status of psychology in society and revealing the evolutionary meaning of practical psychology as a constructive science that has a unique voice of its own in the polyphony of sciences, creating human history in the psychozoic era.

CONCLUSION

We are on the verge of the third millennium. The elapsing twentieth century has become the first century in the history of mankind that became aware of itself as a century of the new psychozoic era. It is the mental activity of mankind that has been elevated to the rank of a geological factor changing the image of the planet.

The recognition of our time as the psychozoic era is due to Vladimir Ivanovich Verandsky. This is not a simple change of conceptions, theories, or ideologies. Something absolutely different is happening - a change of the world.

Just as the representatives of non-classical physics once opened another reality - the strange reality of the microcosm, representatives of the future non-classical psychology and history, following V.I. Vernadsky's will meet a still stranger multitude of mental worlds that densely enmesh our planet.

One may call these worlds "noosphere". (V.I. Vernadsky), "semoishpere" (Yu.M. Lotman), "field of object-related meanings" (A.N. Leontiev), or "personoshpere" (A.A. Ukhtomsky). Each of these names highlights nuances of the special planet's layer that is continuously changing in the psychozoic era. Most important is that this special reality does exist. Researchers collide with it facing paradoxes that are a match for paradoxes of quantum physics and the theory of relativity.

In the historical-evolutionary approach the psychology of personality is viewed as a science, in many respects defining creative evolution in the psychozoic era. This evolution goes along the way of the reproduction of new and new "worlds", most various environments. The creative pulsing of the person may give birth to new cultures and civilizations, other variants for development of humankind, other "environments". Products of these pulsings are Aristotelian rational logic, Euclidean geometrical space, the Cartesian coordinate system, the world of Newtonian classical physics. All these "worlds" are manifestations of the noosphere, originated in the course of scientific evolution and claiming to be the unique classical reality in certain historical periods.

Everybody knows the great formula, "... God created the heaven and the ground". Or the idea that took possession of a part of humankind "... We shall build a new world of our own...". The worlds according to the Bible, the Koran or Marx mythology are hardly less tangible than the world of Newton's classical physics.

Vernadsky's ideas of the psychozoic era change the reference system in considerations about the place of psychology and the role of the psychologist in the historical-evolutionary process of development of nature and society. Which conclusions should psychology draw from the understanding that in the psychozoic era the mind has become a factor of the evolution of the planet? Is it appropriate to raise the issue that in the psychozoic era the evolution of the human species goes through the development of all new and newer environments? Is it absurd to assume that behind the manifestations of individuality, potential possibilities appear of various trajectories of the evolutionary process in which these or those individual ways of life, meaning-related worlds of persogenesis are transformed into social worlds, ways of life for many generations of humankind?

Some temptations lying in wait for psychologists on the verge of the third millennium can be deduced from this reasoning. Will psychology be able to become a designing discipline upholding its own right to participate in the construction of the historical-evolutionary process? Will psychologists take heart to claim the mission of the designers of history? Will they have the courage not only to understand, but to predict, the birth of which worlds can be effected by decisions made at the level of both separate persons and social groups?

In this book an attempt is made to justify the rightfulness of setting up the spectrum of questions raised above following the historical-evolutionary approach in the psychology of personality, and to disclose the evolutionary meaning of the psychology of personality, being understood as the study of the history of a changing person in a changing world.

In many respects, this book reflects the author's professional biography, which, like any life span, represents the history of rejected alternatives. Three complementary stages of this biography can be metaphorically designated as follows: "Psychologist", "Psychopedagogue", "Psychohistorian".

From the position of psychologist in the first six chapters of the book some statements are established which, finally, can be considered as the conclusions of this work. An analysis of problems of personality development in the context of the historical-evolutionary activity theory approach shows that it is especially clear that the ways of studying human beings in the evolution of nature (biogenesis), history of society (sociogenesis) and life span of individuality (persogenesis) until now from three non-crossing lines in psychology, based on the paradigm of classical rational thinking. Therefore, whatever problems of personality development were discussed in this book, the priority was given to the questions, the solution of which permits finding the crossing points of biogenesis and sociogenesis in human persogenesis. Such questions, for example, include questions on the role of "disseminating selection" in the evolution of individual properties of a person, the evolutionary meaning of preadaptive actions of motleys and heretics in the history of culture, assistance as the original cell of persogenesis of the person, etc. At the selection of similar questions, the emphasis was made on the necessity of selecting a new problem field in psychology, rather than on the statement of some completed variants for solution of the problems raised in the historical-evolutionary approach.

From the position of the psychopedagogue trying to show the possibilities for the historical-evolutionary activity theory approach in the appearance of non-traditional education, the final chapter of the book has been written. The role of practical psychology must be considered as a factor of designing and developing variable education, as well as changing of the social status of psychology in the educational sphere in Russia.

The roles of psychopedagogue and psychohistorian overlap in perspective. The psychopedagogue trusts that the road from the totalitarian culture of usefulness, that which suppresses individuality manifestations and begins to agonize in uncertain critical situations of different historical cataclysms - to the culture of dignity, goes through the developing education. It supports the individuality of the person and presents a wide resource of non-standard social actions in periods of different historical episodes and dramas. The psychohistorian gets involved in whirlpools of social politics and tries, as far as possible, to show the consequences and scripts that are caused by these or those solutions, especially when they are made disregarding the mentality that largely determines the performances played in history.

This book is both a fragment of research, and a fragment of life. Surely, as

Alexey Nikolayevich Leontiev often repeated, the person is the only creature in the living world that can be released from the burden of his own biography. The author could try to straighten the past, to replace in a literal sense Marxist philosophy with ambiguous dots or accurately bypass any mention of "Soviet psychology". But that would entail one more small change. It would be then not the author, but someone else constructing the meaning-related world in the psychozoic epoch.

LIST OF THE AUTHOR'S RELATED PUBLICATIONS

MONOGRAPHS AND TEXTBOOKS

Activity and Set. - Moscow. Moscow State University Publishing House, 1979 - 151 p.

Personality as the Subject of Psychological Research. - Moscow. Moscow State University Publishing house, 1984, 105 p.

Principles of Human Memory Organization: Systems-Activity Theory Approach to the Studying of Cognitive Processes.- Moscow. Moscow State University Publishing House, 1985, 103 pages.

Psychology of Individuality: Methodological Foundations of Personality Development in the Historical-Evolutionary Process. - Moscow. Moscow State University Publishing House, 1986, 96 pages.

Psychology of Personality: Principles of General Psychological Analysis. - Moscow. Moscow State University Publishing House, 1990, 367 pages.

Cultural-Historical Psychology and Designing of Worlds. - Moscow; Voronezh. "Institute of practical psychology", 1996, 768 p.

Non-Standard Education in a Changing World: A Cultural-Historical Perspective. Novgorod, 1993, 25 p. (In co-authorship with M.S. Nyrova).

COLLECTIONS OF MATERIALS ON PRACTICAL PSYCHOLOGY ELABORATED AND PUBLISHED BY THE AUTHOR AS EDITOR

Practical Psychology as the Basis of Individualization and Differentiation of Education. Moscow, 1991, 379 pages.

From Practical Psychology - to Developing Education. *Bulletin of Education*, 1995, 1 7.

ARTICLES AND ABSTRACTS

From the Psychophysics of "pure sensations" - to the Psychophysics of "Sensory Tasks". In: *Problems and Methods of Psychophysics.* - Moscow. Moscow State University Publishing House, 1974. (In co-authorship with I.B. Mikhalevskaya).

On the Problem of Set in General and Social Psychology. *Questions of Psychology*, 1 4. (In co-authorship with I.A. Kovalchuk).

On the Hierarchical Structure of Set as an Activity Regulation Mechanism. In: *The Unconscious: its Nature, Functions and Methods of Research.* Vol. 1. Tbilisi: "Metsniereba". 1978.

On the Dynamic Approach to the Psychological Analysis of Activity. *Questions of Psychology*, 1978, 1 1. (In co-authorship with V.A. Petrovsky).

Some Perspectives on Research of Sense Formations of Personality. *Questions of Psychology*, 1979, 1 4. (In co-authorship with B.S. Bratus, B.V. Zeygarnik, V.A. Petrovsky, E.V. Subbotsky, A.U. Kharash, L.S. Tsvetkova).

Principles of Studying Sense Formations of Personality. In: *The Development of Ergonomics in the System of Design.* Borzhomi. 1979. (In co-authorship with A.A. Nasinovskaya, A.Z. Basina).

On the Dependence of the Influence of Need on Behavior from the Place of Need in the Structure of Activity (food deprivation). In: *The Development of Ergonomics in the System of Design.* Borzhomi. 1979. (In co-authorship with S.I. Kuryachy).

The Analysis of Sets in the Situation of Simulation Game. In: *Psychological-Pedagogical Problems of Communication.* Moscow. 1979. (In co-authorship with A.I. Ailamazian).

Classification of Unconscious Phenomena and the Category of Activity. *Questions of Psychology.* 1980, 1 3.

Dispositional Structure of the Regulation of Social Behavior of a Person: From the hypothesis - to the conception. *Questions of Psychology*, 1980, 1 3.

A Burden of Choice. *Young Communist*, 1981, 1 3.

Three Sides of Interiorization. Scientific heritage of L.S. Vygotsky and modern psychology. Moscow. 1981.

Main Principles of the Psychological Analysis in the Activity Theory

Approach. *Questions of Psychology*, 1982, 1 2.

On the Subject of the Psychology of Personality. *Questions of Psychology*, 1983, 1 3.

A review of: A.V.Petrovsky. Personality. Activity. Collective. *Questions of Philosophy*, 1984, 1 7.

The Role of Biological Premises in Personality Development. In: *Psychological Problems of Individuality*, vol.2. Moscow. 1984. (In co-authorship with V.V. Semenov).

National Character and Individuality. In: *Psychological Problems of Individuality*, vol.2. Moscow. 1984. (In co-authorship with A.I. Shliagina).

Premises of the Socioevolutionary Conception of Personality. In: *Experimental Methods of Personality Research in a Collective.* Daugavpils. 1985.

Sociogenetics sources of Personalization. In: *Experimental Methods of Personality Research in a Collective.* Daugavpils. 1985. (In co-authorship with V.V. Abramenkova).

On The Crossroads of Ways of Studying the Human Mind: Unconscious, Set, Activity. In: *The Unconscious: its Nature, Functions and Methods of Research.* Tbilisi, 1985.

On the Understanding of Motive in Present Day Psychology. In: *Psychological-Pedagogical Problems of Motivation of Educational and Labor Activity.* Novosibirsk. 1985. (In co-authorship with A.I. Feigenberg, A.I. Shliagina).

The Role of Social Position in the Reorganization of the Motivational-Sense Sphere in Oncological Patients. *Korsakov Journal of Neuropathology and Psychiatry*, 1985, 1, 12. (In co-authorship with O. Yu. Marilova).

Section of "Psychology of Personality" of the program of course *General Psychology for Psychological Faculties of Universities.* - Moscow. 1985.

Historical-Evolutionary Approach to the Understanding of Personality: Problems and Perspectives for Investigation. *Questions of Psychology*, 1, 1, 1989.

In the Search of the Socio-Evolutionary Conception of Personality Development. (On the Centenary of D.N. Uznadze). Tbilisi. 1986.

Biology and Genetics. The Program for state universities. Specialty 2012 - Psychology. Moscow. 1986. (General editor in co-authorship with B.I. Mednikov. Compilers: N.P. Dubinin, A.Z. Kukarkin).

Cognitive Style as a Means of Resolving Problem and Conflict Situations. In: *Cognitive Styles*. Tallinn. 1986.

Psychological Service and the Tasks of Ethnopsychology. Psychological Science and Practice. Novosibirsk. 1987. (In co-authorship with I.I. Kuznetsov, A.I. Shliagina).

To Be or To Forget: A Psychologist's View on History. Moscow, Pravda, 31.05.1988.

Three Dimensions of the Phenomenon of Personalization of Personality in Sociogenesis. In: *Personality and Interpersonal Relationships in a Collective*. Ulianovsk, 1988. (In co-authorship with V.V. Abramenkova).

Psychology: Looking for the Person. (Round Table of the Institute of Human Studies). Knowledge is Power, 1988, 1, 1. (In co-authorship with I.A. Arthemova, B.S. Bratus, S.N. Enikolopov, A.V. Mudrik, S.A. Smirnov, V.A. Shkuratov).

Create Yourself. (Round Table of the Institute of Human Studies). Knowledge is Power, 1988, 1, 3. (In co-authorship with V.P. Zinchenko, V.A. Petrovsky, V.S. Rotenberg, R.I. Frumkina).

Personality: a Psychological Strategy of Upbringing. In: *New Pedagogical Thinking*. - Moscow. 1989.

Do We Know Ourselves? Unconscious Mechanisms of Behavior Regulation (A brochure). Moscow: Znanie, 1989.

Some Aspects of Nonverbal Communication: Beyond the Threshold of Rationality. *Psychological Journal*, 1989. vol. 10, #6. (In co-authorship with A.I. Feigenberg).

International clubs and all-human values in light of historical ethnopsychology. *Perestroika and the Present Day Club*. Perm. 1989. (In co-authorship with A.I. Shliagina).

Ethnopsychology as a Methodological Basis of the Psychological Service for Interethnic Relationships. The Problem of a Complex Study of Interethnic Relationships in the USSR. Moscow. Moscow State University, 1989. (In co-authorship with A.I. Shliagina).

A Path Not Traveled: From the Culture of Usefulness - to the Culture of Dignity. *Questions of Psychology*, 1990, 1 5.

Activity Theory Approach. Activity. Action. Operation. In: *Psychology: A Dictionary*. 1990.

Motive. Motivation. Motivating. Goal. In: *Psychology: A Dictionary*. 1990.

Personal Sense. In: *Psychology: A Dictionary*. 1990.

Unconscious. Subsensory perception. In: *Psychology: A Dictionary*. 1990.

Postulate of Immediacy. D.N. Uznadze. Set. Theory of set. In: *Psychology: A Dictionary*. 1990.

Emotional Experience. Empathy. In: *Psychology: A Dictionary*. 1990.

Sociogenesis (in psychology). In: *Psychology: A Dictionary*. 1990. (In co-authorship with V.V. Abramenkova).

Unconscious. In: *Philosophical Encyclopedical Dictionary*. 1990.

Motive. In: *Philosophical Encyclopedical Dictionary*. 1990.

Dialogues about the Person Without a Beginning and an End. In: *How to Build your "Self"*. 1991.

At the Sources of Psychoanalytical Pedagogics. In: . Buthner. *To Live with Aggressive Children*. Moscow., 1991.

Lessons of Practical Psychology. *Psychology Today*, 1991, 1, 1.

Psychology of the Person. Teacher's newspaper, on January 1, 1991.

Generation that Attained the Goal. (Round Table of the Institute of Human Studies). Knowledge is Power, 1991, 1, 10. (In co-authorship with B.S. Bratus, V.A. Petrovsky, L.A. Radzikhovsky, V.I. Levin).

Sets of the Person and Illegal Behavior. *Questions of Psychology*. 1991, 1, 2. (In the co-authorship with V.N. Ivanchenko, S.N. Enikolopov).

Education as the Extension of Possibilities of Personality Development: From the selective assessment - to the developmental diagnostics. *Questions of Psychology*, 1992, 1, 1-2. (In the co-authorship with G.A. Yagodin).

Ecology, Psychology and Historical-Evolutionary Approach. Alma Mater. The High School Bulletin. 1992, 1, 1.

School of Uncertainty: Official's Psychoanalytical Notices. Moscow Club, 1993, 1, 3.

Social Biography of the Cultural-Historical Psychology. In: L.S. Vygotsky, A.R. Luria. *Etudes on the History of Behavior*. - Moscow. 1993.

Optimistic Tragedy of a Gifted Child. Knowledge is Power, 1993, 1, 9.

Children's Psychoanalysis. In: *A. Freud. "Ego" and defense mechanisms* . Moscow., 1993.

Psychology, Art and Education. Art at school, 1993, 1, 9.

Personality. In: *Russian Pedagogical Encyclopedia*. 1993. V.1. (In co-authorship with A.V. Petrovsky).

Reforms, Broken at Psychology. In: *Provincial Mentality of Russia in the Past and the Present*. 1994.

Cultural-Historical Psychology and Possibilities of Using Nonverbal

Communication in the Reeducation of Personality. *Questions of Psychology*, 1994, 1 6. (In co-authorship with A.I. Feigenberg).
Strategy of Variable Education: Myths and Reality. Magister. *Independent Psychological-Pedagogical Journal*. 1995, 1, 1.

ARTICLES PUBLISHED IN FOREIGN LANGUAGES

Classification of Unconscious Phenomena and the Category of Activity. *Soviet Psychology*, 1981, vol. 10, No. 3, p. 29-45.
The Subject Matter of the Psychology of Personality. *Soviet Psychology*, 1984, vol. 10, No. 4, p.23-43.
Basic Principles of a Psychological Analysis in the Theory of Activity. *Soviet Psychology*, 1986 -1987, vol. 10, 1 2, p.78-102.
Premises of a Socioevolutionary Concept of the Personality. *Soviet Psychology*, 1987-1988, vol. 10, No. 2, p.51-63.
Activity and Set in Soviet Psychology. Part.I. Multidisciplinary Newsletter for Activity Theory. 1, 5/6, 1990, p.44-51.
Activity and Set in Soviet Psychology. Part.II. Multidisciplinary Newsletter for Activity Theory, 1, 78, 1991, p.41-50.
A la croisee des chemins: etude du psychisme humain (Inconscient, attitude, activite). In: *L'inconscient: la Discussion Continue*. Moscou.1989, p.76-95.
A pszichologiai teve kenyse gelmelet al apelvei. *"Filozofiai Figyelo"*, 1986, 1, 3-4. Budapest, p. 55-64.
El objeto de la psicologia de la personalidad. *Revista de Psiqvitria Y Psicologia Humanista*, 1987, 1, 19-20, Barselona, p.99-111.
L'Aurore esamina il concretto di inconscio e la classificzione dei fenomeni inconsci nello schema di riferimento constituto daiia teoria psicologica dell'attivita. *Studi di psicologia dell'educazione*. 1991, 1, 3. Roma, p.32-40.
Prinzipien und Perspektiven der Analyse der Tatigkeit in der Sowjetischen Psychologie. In: *Internationaler Kongress zur Tatigkeitstheorie*. 2nd Edition. Berlin. 1988, Bd.1, p.7-38. (Mit B.M.Velickovskij).

Index

D

defense mechanisms, 73, 99
deficiency needs, 48, 49, 50
demanding character, 80
depersonalization, 53
depersonalized education, 84
descriptive variables, 44
developing education, 82, 86, 93
deviations, 2, 28, 33, 47, 61, 75, 76, 77, 82
dialogue of cultures, 21, 86
differential psychology, 39, 43, 44
dignity, xiii, xv, 15, 17, 82, 85, 98
dismorphophobia, 52, 53
distortions, 47, 77

E

ecology, 89
economy, 87, 89
education, xiv, xvi, xxvi, xxix, 18, 21, 81,
    82, 83, 84, 85, 86, 87, 88, 89, 90, 93,
    95, 99, 100
education reforms, 83
education system, 82
educational fields, 87, 88
educational institutions, 83, 87, 88, 89
educational process, 89
ego, 54, 87, 89, 99
egocentrism, 4
embryogenesis, 6, 7
emotional excitability, 51
emotionality, 44
endowments, 28, 40, 51, 63
environment, xxii, 3, 5, 9, 11, 26, 29, 30,
    48, 53, 54
equality, 83
ethics, xv, xxiii
ethnic community, 29, 87
ethnic distinctions, 49
ethnic self-consciousness, 63
ethnopsychology, xvi, xxi, 60, 98
eurocentrism, 4, 8
evolutionary regularities, 6, 25, 38

evolutionary snobbery, 4, 7
existential psychology, 72
expectation, 2
exteriorization, 69, 79
extraversion, 51

F

family education, 87
fanatic personality, 66
field of object meanings, 79
folklore, 36, 37, 64
food urges, 50
functional fixation, 79
functional tendencies, 16

G

game, xvi, 32, 44, 64, 66, 76
genetic psychology, 12
goal determination, 15, 24
goal of action, 57
goal orientation, 84
goal setting, xxiii, 36, 64, 73, 74
goals, 27, 36, 46, 50, 67, 73
growth, xxvi, 48, 49, 50, 63, 71, 88
growth needs, 48, 49, 50

H

habituation, 2
heredity, xxii, 3, 29, 30, 53
high school, 88, 89
historical psychology, xxi, xxv, 60
historical time, 59, 61, 62, 63, 66
historical-evolutionary activity, xiv, xv,
    xvi, 78, 93
historical-evolutionary approach, xiii, xiv,
    xv, xix, xxi, xxii, xxv, xxvi, xxvii,
    xxviii, xxix, 11, 16, 21, 23, 25, 31, 35,
    36, 37, 40, 43, 45, 47, 59, 60, 64, 66,
    69, 71, 72, 79, 80, 81, 82, 85, 91, 92,
    93, 97, 99
homeostasis, 10, 11, 30, 49, 50

I

J

K

L

M